Demonstration Problems and Notes

ACCOUNTING PRINCIPLES

16th EDITION

FESS · WARREN

Prepared by
L. PADEN NEELEY, Ph.D., C.P.A.
Professor of Accounting
and President
Professional Development Institute
University of North Texas

AB70QD5
PUBLISHED BY
SOUTH-WESTERN PUBLISHING CO.
CINCINNATI, OH   WEST CHICAGO, IL   DALLAS, TX   LIVERMORE, CA

ISBN: 0-538-80615-X

1 2 3 4 5 6 7 E 4 3 2 1 0 9

Printed in the United States of America

CONTENTS

Notes from lecture and study:

_____
_____
_____
_____
_____
_____
_____
_____
_____
_____
_____
_____
_____
_____
_____
_____
_____
_____
_____
_____
_____
_____
_____
_____
_____

Chapter 1 (Continued)

1. *Effect of transactions on the accounting equation.*

   Lisa Korak is starting a management consulting service in Denver.

   (a) Analyze the following transactions for Korak for the month of July, recording your analysis in the space provided.

   (b) Total each column and make sure assets equal liabilities plus owner's equity.

ASSETS			=	LIABILITIES +		OWNER'S EQUITY
Cash	+ Accounts Receivable	+ Supplies	=	Accounts Payable	+	Korak, Capital
Korak invested $20,000 in the business.						
Paid phone company for installation of office phones, $220. (Installation Expense)						
Paid $1,360 advertising expense.						
Purchased $690 of supplies on account.						
Charged customers for services on account, $4,200.						
Paid office rent expense, $1,250.						
Collected $2,000 previously charged to customers.						
Received $3,920 from cash customers.						
Paid utilities expense for the month, $960.						
Supplies on hand at the end of the month totaled $430.						
Korak withdrew $1,600 for personal use.						
TOTAL						

   (c) Compute the net income earned by Korak for the month. _____

   (d) How much of the income did she retain in the business? _____

2. *Preparing a balance sheet.*

From the following information and using the account form, prepare a balance sheet for the Kam Company as of September 30, 1990.

Accounts Payable	$ 3,680
Accounts Receivable	6,610
Cash	4,480
D. N. Kam, Capital	?
Equipment	8,400
Land	38,000
Notes Payable	4,000
Prepaid Insurance	900
Salaries Payable	1,620
Supplies	560

3. *Effect of transactions on assets and equities; statement preparation.*

(a) On the form provided, record the following changes in assets and equities of Linda Muex's Carpet Cleaning Company that occurred in February of the current year.

1. Muex invested $18,600 in the business.
2. Paid rent expense for month, $850.
3. Paid utility expense, $550.
4. Purchased cleaning supplies on account, $760.
5. Purchased office supplies for cash, $235.

3. *(Cont'd.)*

(a) 6. Charged customers for services on account, $4,475.
    7. Borrowed $3,750 from local bank giving a 60-day note for the balance.
    8. Received $3,225 from cash customers.
    9. Paid $265 to creditor in (4).
  10. Received $2,480 from customers billed in (6).
  11. Paid salary expenses for month, $1,875.
  12. Muex withdrew $615 for personal use.
  13. Determined supplies used during the month as follows: cleaning supplies, $530; office supplies, $75.

Total each account column and make sure the equation balances.

	ASSETS				=	LIABILITIES		+	OWNER'S EQUITY
	Cash	+ Accounts + Receivable	Office Supplies	+ Cleaning Supplies	=	Accounts + Payable	Notes Payable	+	Muex, Capital
1.									
2.									
3.									
4.									
5.									
6.									
7.									
8.									
9.									
10.									
11.									
12.									
13.									
14.									

(b) Prepare an income statement for the Muex Carpet Cleaning Company for February of the current year.

3. *(Cont'd.)*

(c) Prepare a statement of owner's equity of the Muex Carpet Cleaning Company for February of the current year.

(d) Using the account form, prepare a balance sheet for the Muex Carpet Cleaning Company on February 28 of the current year.

4. *Preparing financial statements for a corporation.*

Below you are given the amounts of the Rodriquez Corporation's assets, liabilities, and capital stock as of September 30, 1990, and the revenue and expenses for the year ended on that date. Rodriquez had retained earnings of $24,810 on October 1, 1989, the beginning of the current year. During the current year, the corporation paid cash dividends of $20,500.

Cash	$ 16,410
Accounts receivable	91,300
Office supplies	810
Prepaid insurance	1,800
Land	150,000
Accounts payable	17,100
Notes payable	4,000
Salaries payable	2,210
Taxes payable	3,900
Capital stock	150,000
Fees earned	225,300
Advertising expense	6,600
Rent expense	18,000
Salary expense	81,700
Office supplies expense	3,400
Taxes expense	13,400
Utilities expense	19,200
Insurance expense	4,200

(a) Prepare an income statement for the Rodriquez Corporation for the year ended September 30, 1990.

4. *(Cont'd.)*

(b) Prepare a retained earnings statement for the Rodriquez Cororation for the year ended September 30, 1990.

(c) Using the report form, prepare a balance sheet for the Rodriquez Corporation as of September 30, 1990.

Chapter 1 (Continued)

5. *Analyzing a statement of owner's equity and a statement of retained earnings.*

Complete the following missing link problems by placing the correct amounts in the blanks provided.

STATEMENT OF OWNER'S EQUITY

	Case P	Case D	Case I
Owner's equity 1-1-90	16,700	13,400	27,600
Additional investment	2,900	_____	1,600
Net income (loss)	_____	(1,400)	4,100
Withdrawals	1,500	1,800	1,100
Owner's equity 1-31-90	16,200	10,400	_____

RETAINED EARNINGS STATEMENT

	Case U	Case N	Case T
Retained earnings 1-1-90	_____	33,600	19,500
Net income (loss)	(2,500)	19,600	_____
Dividends	2,000	8,000	4,000
Retained earnings 1-31-90	12,900	_____	22,600

Notes from lecture and study:

_____

_____

_____

_____

_____

_____

_____

_____

_____

_____

_____

_____

_____

_____

_____

_____

_____

_____

_____

_____

_____

_____

_____

Chapter 2 (Continued)

1. *Recording and analyzing transactions; preparing a trial balance.*

   (a) In the T accounts below, indicate on the line provided if a debit to that account is an increase (+) or a decrease (−); also indicate the effect of a credit on each account by + or −.

Cash	Accounts Receivable	Accounts Payable	Notes Payable

Cleaning Supplies	Cleaning Equipment	Lehman, Capital	Lehman, Drawing

Capital Stock	Retained Earnings	Expenses	Cleaning Revenue

1. *(Cont'd.)*

(b) Analyze the following transactions for Lehman's Cleaners for the month of November, and record debit and credit amounts in the T accounts set up in (a).

1. Lehman invested $20,000 cash in the business.
2. Purchased cleaning equipment for $24,000, paying $8,000 and giving an 8-month note for the balance.
3. Purchased $680 cleaning supplies on account.
4. Charged customers for services on account, $3,200.
5. Received $1,920 from cash customers.
6. Paid $2,300 expenses.
7. Received $1,900 from customers billed in (4).
8. Paid $400 to creditor in (3).
9. Lehman withdrew $800 for personal use.

(c) Prepare a trial balance for Lehman's Cleaners from the previous T accounts after all transactions have been recorded on November 30.

Chapter 2 (Continued)

2. *Classifying accounts.*

For each account listed below, indicate the financial statement on which it would be shown; if it is a balance sheet account, indicate the section where it would appear (i.e., current assets, current liabilities, etc.). Also indicate the normal balance of the account (debit or credit).

Account	Statement	Section	Normal Balance
(0) Cash	Balance Sheet	Current Assets	Debit
(a) Accounts Payable			
(b) Accounts Receivable			
(c) Advertising Expense			
(d) Buildings			
(e) Capital Stock			
(f) Delivery Equipment			
(g) Depreciation Expense			
(h) Dividends			
(i) Fees Earned			
(j) Insurance Expense			
(k) Interest Payable			
(l) Land			
(m) Machinery			
(n) Mortgage Payable			
(o) Notes Payable (30 days)			
(p) Notes Payable (5 years)			
(q) Notes Receivable (3 mo.)			
(r) Prepaid Rent			
(s) Retained Earnings			
(t) Salaries Payable			
(u) Sales			
(v) Store Supplies			
(w) Supplies Expense			
(x) Taxes Payable			
(y) Utilities Expense			

3. *Journalizing.*

Record the transactions for Lehman's Cleaners in Problem 1 in the following two-column journal. Use the transaction number for the date.

JOURNAL

	DATE		DESCRIPTION	POST. REF.	DEBIT	CREDIT	
1							1
2							2
3							3
4							4
5							5
6							6
7							7
8							8
9							9
10							10
11							11
12							12
13							13
14							14
15							15
16							16
17							17
18							18
19							19
20							20
21							21
22							22
23							23
24							24
25							25
26							26
27							27
28							28
29							29
30							30

PAGE

4. *Journalizing, posting, and preparing a trial balance.*

The Geneva Corporation is a graphics design firm organized in Albuquerque, New Mexico.

(a) Record the following transactions for the month of May for Geneva Corporation in the two-column general journal provided.

May   1. Geneva sold $75,000 of capital stock for cash.

      3. Purchased a light table and other design equipment for $6,300 on account.

      3. Purchased supplies for cash, $460.

      5. Paid for ads in local newspaper, $750.

      7. Charged customers for services on account, $2,500 (Design Revenue).

      9. Paid $1,600 to creditors.

    12. Purchased supplies on account, $260.

    16. Received design revenue from cash customers, $2,050.

    24. Received $1,040 from customers on account.

    26. Charged customers for services on account, $2,280.

    29. Paid salaries for month, $1,680.

    30. Supplies used during month, $420.

    31. Issued an additional $10,000 of capital stock for cash.

4. *(Cont'd.)*

(a)

| | JOURNAL | | | | PAGE **2** |

	DATE		DESCRIPTION	POST. REF.	DEBIT	CREDIT	
1							1
2							2
3							3
4							4
5							5
6							6
7							7
8							8
9							9
10							10
11							11
12							12
13							13
14							14
15							15
16							16
17							17
18							18
19							19
20							20
21							21
22							22
23							23
24							24
25							25
26							26
27							27
28							28
29							29
30							30
31							31

Chapter 2 (Continued)

4. *(Cont'd.)*

(b) Post the journal entries to the ledger.

ACCOUNT **Cash**   ACCOUNT NO. **11**

DATE		ITEM	POST. REF.	DEBIT	CREDIT	BALANCE DEBIT	BALANCE CREDIT

ACCOUNT **Accounts Receivable**   ACCOUNT NO. **12**

DATE		ITEM	POST. REF.	DEBIT	CREDIT	BALANCE DEBIT	BALANCE CREDIT

ACCOUNT **Supplies**   ACCOUNT NO. **17**

DATE		ITEM	POST. REF.	DEBIT	CREDIT	BALANCE DEBIT	BALANCE CREDIT

ACCOUNT **Design Equipment**   ACCOUNT NO. **27**

DATE		ITEM	POST. REF.	DEBIT	CREDIT	BALANCE DEBIT	BALANCE CREDIT

ACCOUNT **Accounts Payable**   ACCOUNT NO. **31**

DATE		ITEM	POST. REF.	DEBIT	CREDIT	BALANCE DEBIT	BALANCE CREDIT

4. *(Cont'd.)*

(b)

ACCOUNT **Capital Stock**   ACCOUNT NO. **41**

DATE	ITEM	POST. REF.	DEBIT	CREDIT	BALANCE	
					DEBIT	CREDIT

ACCOUNT **Retained Earnings**   ACCOUNT NO. **42**

DATE	ITEM	POST. REF.	DEBIT	CREDIT	BALANCE	
					DEBIT	CREDIT

ACCOUNT **Design Revenue**   ACCOUNT NO. **51**

DATE	ITEM	POST. REF.	DEBIT	CREDIT	BALANCE	
					DEBIT	CREDIT

ACCOUNT **Salary Expense**   ACCOUNT NO. **61**

DATE	ITEM	POST. REF.	DEBIT	CREDIT	BALANCE	
					DEBIT	CREDIT

ACCOUNT **Advertising Expense**   ACCOUNT NO. **64**

DATE	ITEM	POST. REF.	DEBIT	CREDIT	BALANCE	
					DEBIT	CREDIT

ACCOUNT **Supplies Expense**   ACCOUNT NO. **67**

DATE	ITEM	POST. REF.	DEBIT	CREDIT	BALANCE	
					DEBIT	CREDIT

4. *(Cont'd.)*

(c) Prepare a trial balance for Geneva Corporation as of May 31.

5. *Analyzing errors in the trial balance.*

Explain the effect of the following errors on the trial balance (Will it be out of balance? What will the effect be on the total debits? total credits?). Consider each error independently.

(a) A debit to Utility Expense for $210 was posted as $120.

_____
_____
_____

_____

(b) Sales on account of $510 were recorded as a debit to Cash for $510 and a credit to Sales for $510.

_____
_____

_____

_____

(c) A credit of $300 to Accounts Receivable was not posted.

_____
_____
_____

_____

(d) A debit of $400 to supplies was posted twice.

_____
_____

_____

_____

(e) Purchase of office supplies for $260 cash; posted as a debit to Office Supplies, $260, and a credit to Cash, $26.

_____
_____

_____

_____

Chapter 3   COMPLETION OF THE ACCOUNTING CYCLE

Notes from lecture and study:

_____
_____
_____
_____
_____
_____
_____
_____
_____
_____
_____
_____
_____
_____
_____
_____
_____
_____
_____
_____
_____
_____
_____
_____
_____
_____

1. *Making adjusting entries.*

(a) The following information is found in the accounts of Brock's Billboard Company. Assuming Brock prepared quarterly financial statements, what adjusting entry would be required March 31?

ACCOUNT **Prepaid Insurance**   ACCOUNT NO. **16**

DATE		ITEM	POST. REF.	DEBIT	CREDIT	BALANCE	
						DEBIT	CREDIT
19-- Jan.	1	Payment for 12 months	27	4 8 0 0 00		4 8 0 0 00	

JOURNAL   PAGE **30**

	DATE		DESCRIPTION	POST. REF.	DEBIT	CREDIT	
1							1
2							2
3							3

(b) During the quarter, office supplies were purchased for $725 cash. A count of office supplies on hand at the end of the quarter totaled $260. Prepare the journal entries necessary to (1) record the purchase of the supplies, (2) make the necessary adjustment at the end of the month, and (3) post the entries to the ledger accounts given.

ACCOUNT **Office Supplies**   ACCOUNT NO. **14**

DATE		ITEM	POST. REF.	DEBIT	CREDIT	BALANCE	
						DEBIT	CREDIT

ACCOUNT **Office Supplies Expense**   ACCOUNT NO. **54**

DATE		ITEM	POST. REF.	DEBIT	CREDIT	BALANCE	
						DEBIT	CREDIT

1. *(Cont'd.)*

(c) A new microcomputer was purchased by Brock's Billboard Company on April 1 for $5,400 cash. The depreciation on the microcomputer from April through December 31 was $920. Prepare the entries to record the purchase of the microcomputer and the adjusting entry on December 31. Post the entries to the ledger accounts given.

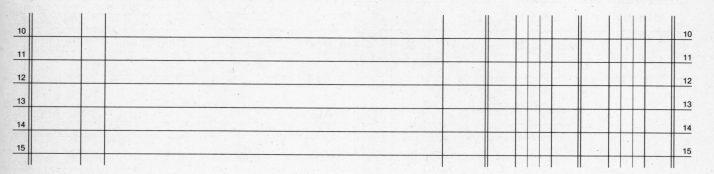

ACCOUNT **Microcomputer**   ACCOUNT NO. **19**

DATE	ITEM	POST. REF.	DEBIT	CREDIT	BALANCE DEBIT	BALANCE CREDIT

ACCOUNT **Accumulated Depreciation—Microcomputer**   ACCOUNT NO. **19.1**

DATE	ITEM	POST. REF.	DEBIT	CREDIT	BALANCE DEBIT	BALANCE CREDIT

ACCOUNT **Depreciation Expense—Microcomputer**   ACCOUNT NO. **59**

DATE	ITEM	POST. REF.	DEBIT	CREDIT	BALANCE DEBIT	BALANCE CREDIT

(d) The weekly pay period for Brock's Billboard Company ends on Friday and totals $3,060 per week for a five-day period. The last day of the fiscal year falls on Tuesday. Prepare the adjusting entry for accrued salaries on December 31.

2. *Closing entries.*

The capital, drawing, revenue, and expense accounts for Fu Advertising Service at the end of the year after all adjustments have been made and posted are given below. Prepare journal entries to close the books on page 24 and post to the ledger accounts.

ACCOUNT **Dan Fu, Capital** ACCOUNT NO. **31**

DATE		ITEM	POST. REF.	DEBIT	CREDIT	BALANCE	
						DEBIT	CREDIT
19-- Dec.	31		✔				14 0 8 0 0 00

ACCOUNT **Dan Fu, Drawing** ACCOUNT NO. **32**

DATE		ITEM	POST. REF.	DEBIT	CREDIT	BALANCE	
						DEBIT	CREDIT
19-- Dec.	31					1 4 4 0 0 00	

ACCOUNT **Income Summary** ACCOUNT NO. **33**

DATE		ITEM	POST. REF.	DEBIT	CREDIT	BALANCE	
						DEBIT	CREDIT

ACCOUNT **Service Fees** ACCOUNT NO. **41**

DATE		ITEM	POST. REF.	DEBIT	CREDIT	BALANCE	
						DEBIT	CREDIT
19-- Dec.	31		✔				11 2 8 0 0 00

ACCOUNT **Salary Expense** ACCOUNT NO. **51**

DATE		ITEM	POST. REF.	DEBIT	CREDIT	BALANCE	
						DEBIT	CREDIT
19-- Dec.	31					3 3 2 0 0 00	

ACCOUNT **Rent Expense** ACCOUNT NO. **52**

DATE		ITEM	POST. REF.	DEBIT	CREDIT	BALANCE	
						DEBIT	CREDIT
19-- Dec.	31					3 6 0 0 0 00	

2. *(Cont'd.)*

ACCOUNT **Depreciation Expense**   ACCOUNT NO. **54**

DATE		ITEM	POST. REF.	DEBIT	CREDIT	BALANCE	
						DEBIT	CREDIT
19-- Dec.	31		✓			8 4 0 0 00	

ACCOUNT **Utilities Expense**   ACCOUNT NO. **55**

DATE		ITEM	POST. REF.	DEBIT	CREDIT	BALANCE	
						DEBIT	CREDIT
19-- Dec.	31		✓			2 8 8 0 0 00	

JOURNAL   PAGE **26**

	DATE		DESCRIPTION	POST. REF.	DEBIT	CREDIT	
1							1
2							2
3							3
4							4
5							5
6							6
7							7
8							8
9							9
10							10
11							11
12							12
13							13
14							14
15							15
16							16
17							17
18							18
19							19
20							20
21							21

3. *Preparing a work sheet and financial statements.*

The trial balance of Hughes Flight School on December 31, the end of the current fiscal year, is recorded in the ten-column work sheet on the following page. Data for adjustments are as follows:

Office supplies on hand on December 31	$ 410
Depreciation for the year	4,230
Insurance expired during the year	1,260
Salaries accrued on December 31	3,330

(a) Complete the work sheet for Hughes Flight School.

(b) Prepare an income statement for the year in the space below.

Chapter 3 (Continued)

3. *(Cont'd.)*

(a)

Hughes Flight School
Work Sheet
For Year Ended December 31, 19--

ACCOUNT TITLE	ACCT. NO.	TRIAL BALANCE DEBIT	TRIAL BALANCE CREDIT	ADJUSTMENTS DEBIT	ADJUSTMENTS CREDIT	ADJUSTED TRIAL BALANCE DEBIT	ADJUSTED TRIAL BALANCE CREDIT	INCOME STATEMENT DEBIT	INCOME STATEMENT CREDIT	BALANCE SHEET DEBIT	BALANCE SHEET CREDIT
1 Cash		1 6 3 0 00									
2 Office Supplies		1 3 2 5 00									
3 Prepaid Insurance		1 9 5 0 00									
4 Office Equipment		32 0 0 0 00									
5 Accumulated Depreciation			6 2 0 0 00								
6 Accounts Payable			1 4 6 0 00								
7 Notes Payable—Bank			3 0 0 0 00								
8 Linda Hughes, Capital			20 1 4 5 00								
9 Linda Hughes, Drawing		15 0 0 0 00									
10 Flight Revenue			84 4 0 0 00								
11 Salary Expense		36 8 0 0 00									
12 Rent Expense		12 6 0 0 00									
13 Utilities Expense		9 8 0 0 00									
14 Advertising Expense		4 1 0 0 00									
15		115 2 0 5 00	115 2 0 5 00								

3. *(Cont'd.)*

(c) Prepare a statement of owner's equity and a balance sheet for the year ended December 31 for Hughes Flight School.

Chapter 3 (Continued)

4. *Adjusting entries, closing entries, and post-closing trial balance.*

The ledger accounts for Hughes Flight School at the end of the year before adjustments have been made are given below.

(a) Prepare journal entries to record the adjusting entries for Hughes Flight School on page 31, and post to the ledger accounts.

(b) Prepare entries to close the books on page 31, and post to the ledger accounts.

(c) Prepare a post-closing trial balance on page 32.

ACCOUNT **Cash** ACCOUNT NO. **11**

DATE		ITEM	POST. REF.	DEBIT	CREDIT	BALANCE	
						DEBIT	CREDIT
19-- Dec.	31		✓			1 6 3 0 00	

ACCOUNT **Office Supplies** ACCOUNT NO. **14**

DATE		ITEM	POST. REF.	DEBIT	CREDIT	BALANCE	
						DEBIT	CREDIT
19-- Dec.	31		✓			1 3 2 5 00	

ACCOUNT **Prepaid Insurance** ACCOUNT NO. **15**

DATE		ITEM	POST. REF.	DEBIT	CREDIT	BALANCE	
						DEBIT	CREDIT
19-- Dec.	31		✓			1 9 5 0 00	

ACCOUNT **Office Equipment** ACCOUNT NO. **19**

DATE		ITEM	POST. REF.	DEBIT	CREDIT	BALANCE	
						DEBIT	CREDIT
19-- Dec.	31		✓			32 0 0 0 00	

ACCOUNT **Accumulated Depreciation** ACCOUNT NO. **19.1**

DATE		ITEM	POST. REF.	DEBIT	CREDIT	BALANCE	
						DEBIT	CREDIT
19-- Dec.	31		✓				6 2 0 0 00

ACCOUNT **Accounts Payable** ACCOUNT NO. **21**

DATE		ITEM	POST. REF.	DEBIT	CREDIT	BALANCE	
						DEBIT	CREDIT
19-- Dec.	31		✓				1 4 6 0 00

4. *(Cont'd.)*

ACCOUNT **Notes Payable—Bank**   ACCOUNT NO. **22**

DATE	ITEM	POST. REF.	DEBIT	CREDIT	BALANCE DEBIT	BALANCE CREDIT
19-- Dec. 31		✔				3 0 0 0 00

ACCOUNT **Salaries Payable**   ACCOUNT NO. **23**

DATE	ITEM	POST. REF.	DEBIT	CREDIT	BALANCE DEBIT	BALANCE CREDIT

ACCOUNT **Linda Hughes, Capital**   ACCOUNT NO. **31**

DATE	ITEM	POST. REF.	DEBIT	CREDIT	BALANCE DEBIT	BALANCE CREDIT
19-- Dec. 31		✔				20 1 4 5 00

ACCOUNT **Linda Hughes, Drawing**   ACCOUNT NO. **32**

DATE	ITEM	POST. REF.	DEBIT	CREDIT	BALANCE DEBIT	BALANCE CREDIT
19-- Dec. 31		✔			15 0 0 0 00	

ACCOUNT **Income Summary**   ACCOUNT NO. **33**

DATE	ITEM	POST. REF.	DEBIT	CREDIT	BALANCE DEBIT	BALANCE CREDIT

ACCOUNT **Flight Revenue**   ACCOUNT NO. **41**

DATE	ITEM	POST. REF.	DEBIT	CREDIT	BALANCE DEBIT	BALANCE CREDIT
19-- Dec. 31		✔				84 4 0 0 00

Chapter 3 (Continued)

4. *(Cont'd.)*

ACCOUNT **Salary Expense**   ACCOUNT NO. **51**

DATE		ITEM	POST. REF.	DEBIT	CREDIT	BALANCE	
						DEBIT	CREDIT
19-- Dec.	31		✓			36 8 0 0 00	

ACCOUNT **Rent Expense**   ACCOUNT NO. **52**

DATE		ITEM	POST. REF.	DEBIT	CREDIT	BALANCE	
						DEBIT	CREDIT
19-- Dec.	31		✓			12 6 0 0 00	

ACCOUNT **Utilities Expense**   ACCOUNT NO. **53**

DATE		ITEM	POST. REF.	DEBIT	CREDIT	BALANCE	
						DEBIT	CREDIT
19-- Dec.	31		✓			9 8 0 0 00	

ACCOUNT **Depreciation Expense**   ACCOUNT NO. **54**

DATE		ITEM	POST. REF.	DEBIT	CREDIT	BALANCE	
						DEBIT	CREDIT

ACCOUNT **Advertising Expense**   ACCOUNT NO. **55**

DATE		ITEM	POST. REF.	DEBIT	CREDIT	BALANCE	
						DEBIT	CREDIT
19-- Dec.	31		✓			4 1 0 0 00	

ACCOUNT **Office Supplies Expense**   ACCOUNT NO. **56**

DATE		ITEM	POST. REF.	DEBIT	CREDIT	BALANCE	
						DEBIT	CREDIT

4. *(Cont'd.)*

ACCOUNT **Insurance Expense**   ACCOUNT NO. **57**

DATE		ITEM	POST. REF.	DEBIT	CREDIT	BALANCE	
						DEBIT	CREDIT

JOURNAL   PAGE **3**

	DATE		DESCRIPTION	POST. REF.	DEBIT	CREDIT	
1							1
2							2
3							3
4							4
5							5
6							6
7							7
8							8
9							9
10							10
11							11
12							12
13							13
14							14
15							15
16							16
17							17
18							18
19							19
20							20
21							21
22							22
23							23
24							24
25							25
26							26

4. *(Cont'd.)*

Notes from lecture and study:

Chapter 4 (Continued)

1. *Recording merchandise transactions, returns and allowances, and discounts on the books of the buyer and seller.*

On October 3, Ted Ellis buys merchandise from Joe Henderson at a list price of $9,500 and credit terms of 4/10, n/30. On October 7, Ellis returns damaged merchandise to Henderson for a price of $3,000. Ellis pays the balance of his account on October 12.

(a) Prepare the entries, in general journal form, to record the three transactions on Ellis' books.

JOURNAL

PAGE

	DATE	DESCRIPTION	POST. REF.	DEBIT	CREDIT	
1						1
2						2
3						3
4						4
5						5
6						6
7						7
8						8
9						9

(b) Prepare the necessary entries on Henderson's books.

JOURNAL

PAGE

	DATE	DESCRIPTION	POST. REF.	DEBIT	CREDIT	
1						1
2						2
3						3
4						4
5						5
6						6
7						7
8						8
9						9

(c) Prepare the entry on Ellis' books on October 3 assuming the merchandise is shipped FOB shipping point with prepaid transportation costs of $180 added to the invoice.

10						10
11						11
12						12

1. *(Cont'd.)*

(d) Prepare the entry on Ellis' books on October 12 to record payment of the invoice in (c). There were no damaged goods.

13				13
14				14
15				15

2. *Computing cash discounts.*

(a) Compute the cash discount and amount paid by David's Cycle Shop for each of the following invoices.

Date of Invoice	List Price	Credit Terms	Date Paid	Cash Discount	Amount Paid
May 7	$12,000	n/eom	May 30	_____	_____
May 12	16,000	4/10,n/30	May 21	_____	_____
May 18	26,500	2/10,n/30	May 30	_____	_____
May 25	10,200	3/20,n/60	June 13	_____	_____
May 31	14,000	2/15,n/30	June 18	_____	_____

(b) Assuming David bought the merchandise on May 12 from Johnston Company, give the entries required, in general journal form, to record the transactions on the following dates on David's books.

JOURNAL

PAGE

	DATE		DESCRIPTION	POST. REF.	DEBIT	CREDIT	
1	19-- May	12					1
2							2
3							3
4	19-- May	21					4
5							5
6							6
7							7
8							8
9							9
10							10
11							11
12							12
13							13
14							14

Chapter 4 (Continued)

2. *(Cont'd.)*

    (c) Assuming David sold the merchandise on May 25 to the Nebraska Company, give the entries required, in general journal form, to record the transactions on the following dates on David's books.

15					15
16	19-- May	25			16
17					17
18					18
19	19-- June	13			19
20					20
21					21

3. *Recording sales taxes.*

    (a) Redfern's Luggage Shop operates in a state with a sales tax of 6%. Record a credit sale of $150 plus tax to Kathy Belcher on April 9 and collection of the receivable on April 23 on the books of Redfern.

JOURNAL
PAGE

	DATE		DESCRIPTION	POST. REF.	DEBIT	CREDIT	
1							1
2							2
3							3
4							4
5							5
6							6
7							7

    (b) Record the purchase of the merchandise and payment in (a) above on the books of Kathy Belcher.

JOURNAL
PAGE

	DATE		DESCRIPTION	POST. REF.	DEBIT	CREDIT	
1							1
2							2
3							3
4							4
5							5
6							6

4. *Computing cost of merchandise sold.*

Lee Wong purchased $73,800 of merchandise during the current year. Determine the cost of merchandise sold for the period for each of the following cases. (Consider each one independently.)

(a) There was no inventory on hand at the beginning of the period, but there was $15,400 of goods on hand at the end of the period.

(b) There was $16,420 of merchandise in stock at the beginning of the year and $14,380 on hand at the end of the year.

(c) There was $15,300 of merchandise on hand at the beginning of the year. Purchases discounts totaled $1,220 during the period, and $1,860 of purchases were returned. Inventory at the end of the year totaled $16,720. Wong paid $5,500 in transportation costs during the year.

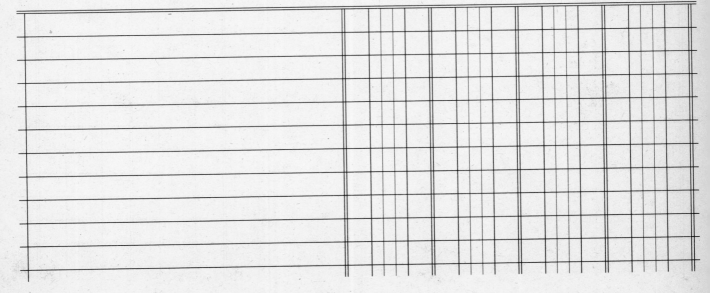

Chapter 4 (Continued)

5. *Adjusting entries for merchandise inventory.*

The merchandise inventory and income summary accounts for Toone Music Shop are presented below. Toone's inventory on December 31 is $24,500.

(a) Prepare the adjusting entries for merchandise inventory at the end of the year.

(b) Post the entries to the ledger accounts.

ACCOUNT   **Merchandise Inventory**   ACCOUNT NO. **13**

DATE		ITEM	POST. REF.	DEBIT	CREDIT	BALANCE	
						DEBIT	CREDIT
19-- Jan.	1		✓			27 4 4 0 00	

ACCOUNT   **Income Summary**   ACCOUNT NO. **33**

DATE	ITEM	POST. REF.	DEBIT	CREDIT	BALANCE	
					DEBIT	CREDIT

JOURNAL   PAGE **13**

	DATE	DESCRIPTION	POST. REF.	DEBIT	CREDIT	
1						1
2						2
3						3
4						4
5						5
6						6
7						7
8						8
9						9
10						10
11						11
12						12
13						13
14						14
15						15
16						16

6. *Recording and posting prepaid expense.*

Cross Camping Supplies decides to start an extensive advertising campaign and arranges with *Outdoor Sportsman Magazine* to take a full-page ad in each of the next 12 issues. The ads will start with the August issue and will cost $3,000 each. Cross pays *Outdoor Sportsman Magazine* the full amount of $36,000 on August 1. The fiscal year for both organizations ends December 31.

(a) Prepare the entries on the books of Cross Camping Supplies to record payment of the advertising and to adjust and close the books on December 31 assuming the payment was debited to the prepaid advertising account. Also record the reversing entry on January 1 if required.

JOURNAL

	DATE	DESCRIPTION	POST. REF.	DEBIT	CREDIT	
1						1
2						2
3						3
4						4
5						5
6						6
7						7
8						8
9						9
10						10
11						11
12						12

Post each entry as it is recorded to the following accounts.

ACCOUNT **Prepaid Advertising** ACCOUNT NO. **119**

DATE	ITEM	POST. REF.	DEBIT	CREDIT	BALANCE DEBIT	BALANCE CREDIT

ACCOUNT **Advertising Expense** ACCOUNT NO. **719**

DATE	ITEM	POST. REF.	DEBIT	CREDIT	BALANCE DEBIT	BALANCE CREDIT

6. *(Cont'd.)*

(b) Prepare the same entries for Cross Camping Supplies as in (a) assuming the initial payment was debited to the advertising expense account.

JOURNAL
PAGE 7

DATE	DESCRIPTION	POST. REF.	DEBIT	CREDIT
1				
2				
3				
4				
5				
6				
7				
8				
9				
10				
11				
12				
13				

Post each entry.

ACCOUNT **Prepaid Advertising** ACCOUNT NO. 119

DATE	ITEM	POST. REF.	DEBIT	CREDIT	BALANCE DEBIT	BALANCE CREDIT

ACCOUNT **Advertising Expense** ACCOUNT NO. 719

DATE	ITEM	POST. REF.	DEBIT	CREDIT	BALANCE DEBIT	BALANCE CREDIT

7. *Recording and posting unearned revenue.*

(a) Prepare the entries on the books of *Outdoor Sportsman Magazine* to record receipt of the $36,000 payment on August 1 from Cross Camping Supplies in Problem 6 and to adjust and close the books on December 31 assuming the receipt was credited to the unearned advertising account. Also prepare the reversing entry on January 1 if required.

JOURNAL

PAGE 11

	DATE		DESCRIPTION	POST. REF.	DEBIT	CREDIT	
1							1
2							2
3							3
4							4
5							5
6							6
7							7
8							8
9							9
10							10
11							11
12							12

Post each entry to the following accounts.

ACCOUNT **Unearned Advertising**   ACCOUNT NO. **243**

DATE	ITEM	POST. REF.	DEBIT	CREDIT	BALANCE DEBIT	BALANCE CREDIT

ACCOUNT **Advertising Income**   ACCOUNT NO. **513**

DATE	ITEM	POST. REF.	DEBIT	CREDIT	BALANCE DEBIT	BALANCE CREDIT

Chapter 4 (Continued)

7. *(Cont'd.)*

(b) Prepare the same entries for *Outdoor Sportsman Magazine* as in (a) assuming the initial payment was credited to the advertising income account.

JOURNAL

	DATE	DESCRIPTION	POST. REF.	DEBIT	CREDIT	
1						1
2						2
3						3
4						4
5						5
6						6
7						7
8						8
9						9
10						10
11						11
12						12
13						13

Post each entry.

ACCOUNT **Unearned Advertising** ACCOUNT NO. **243**

DATE	ITEM	POST. REF.	DEBIT	CREDIT	BALANCE	
					DEBIT	CREDIT

ACCOUNT **Advertising Income** ACCOUNT NO. **513**

DATE	ITEM	POST. REF.	DEBIT	CREDIT	BALANCE	
					DEBIT	CREDIT

8. *Recording accrued income.*

On November 1, 19--, Tracy Helicopter Service rented a helicopter to Chris Executive Services. The rent was $900 per month, payable quarterly. On December 31, the following ledger accounts were provided before adjustment.

ACCOUNT **Rent Receivable**   ACCOUNT NO. **13**

DATE	ITEM	POST. REF.	DEBIT	CREDIT	BALANCE DEBIT	BALANCE CREDIT

ACCOUNT **Rent Income**   ACCOUNT NO. **63**

DATE	ITEM	POST. REF.	DEBIT	CREDIT	BALANCE DEBIT	BALANCE CREDIT

(a) Prepare the adjustment necessary on Tracy's books on December 31 and post.

JOURNAL   PAGE **22**

	DATE	DESCRIPTION	POST. REF.	DEBIT	CREDIT	
1						1
2						2
3						3

(b) Prepare the entry necessary to close Rent Income on December 31 and post.

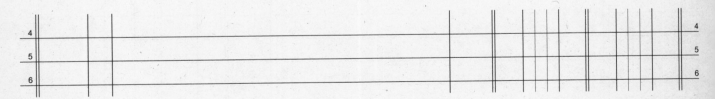

(c) Journalize the entry on January 31 when Tracy receives payment of the quarterly rent and post.

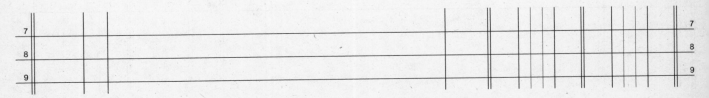

9. *Work sheet, adjusting entries, and partial income statement.*

The work sheet for Guzman Framing Shop as of December 31 of the current year is given on the following page. The adjustment data needed for month-end adjustments are presented below.

Adjustment data:

(a), (b) Merchandise inventory, December 31, $81,200.

(c) Office supplies on hand, December 31, $600.

(d) Rent expired during the month, $12,000.

(e) Depreciation of store equipment, $1,750.

(f) Salaries owed on December 31, $900.

Required:

(a) Complete the ten-column work sheet for the month ended December 31.

(b) Record the adjusting entries in the general journal below.

(c) Prepare the cost of merchandise sold section of the income statement from the data presented in the income statement columns of the work sheet; use the form on page 46.

JOURNAL

PAGE _____

	DATE		DESCRIPTION	POST. REF.	DEBIT	CREDIT	
1							1
2							2
3							3
4							4
5							5
6							6
7							7
8							8
9							9
10							10
11							11
12							12
13							13
14							14
15							15
16							16
17							17
18							18
19							19

9. *(Cont'd.)*

(a)

Guzman Framing Shop
Work Sheet
For Month Ended December 31, 19--

	ACCT. NO.	TRIAL BALANCE DEBIT	TRIAL BALANCE CREDIT	ADJUSTMENTS DEBIT	ADJUSTMENTS CREDIT	ADJUSTED TRIAL BALANCE DEBIT	ADJUSTED TRIAL BALANCE CREDIT	INCOME STATEMENT DEBIT	INCOME STATEMENT CREDIT	BALANCE SHEET DEBIT	BALANCE SHEET CREDIT
1 Cash		20 9 0 0 00									
2 Accounts Receivable		25 7 0 0 00									
3 Merchandise Inventory		83 4 0 0 00									
4 Office Supplies		2 1 5 0 00									
5 Prepaid Rent		18 0 0 0 00									
6 Store Equipment		42 0 0 0 00									
7 Accumulated Depreciation—Store											
8 Equipment			11 5 0 0 00								
9 Accounts Payable			19 3 5 0 00								
10 Jose Guzman, Capital			120 9 0 0 00								
11 Jose Guzman, Drawing		4 0 0 0 00									
12 Sales			158 2 9 0 00								
13 Sales Returns and Allowances		2 2 0 0 00									
14 Sales Discounts		3 1 8 0 00									
15 Purchases		88 1 6 0 00									
16 Purchases Returns and Allowances			2 0 5 0 00								
17 Purchases Discounts			1 8 5 0 00								
18 Transportation In		9 6 0 0 00									
19 Advertising Expense		1 9 0 0 00									
20 Salary Expense		12 0 0 0 00									
21 Utilities Expense		7 5 0 00									
22		313 9 4 0 00	313 9 4 0 00								

9. *(Cont'd.)*

(c)

Notes from lecture and study:

1. *Financial statements for a corporation; closing entries.*

The Income Statement and Balance Sheet columns from the work sheet of the J-Pat Fan Corporation for the year ended December 31 of the current year are shown below.

J-Pat Fan Corporation

Work Sheet

For Year Ended December 31, 19--

	ACCOUNT TITLE	INCOME STATEMENT DEBIT	INCOME STATEMENT CREDIT	BALANCE SHEET DEBIT	BALANCE SHEET CREDIT	
1	Cash			52 000 00		1
2	Accounts Receivable			208 000 00		2
3	Merchandise Inventory			193 000 00		3
4	Store Supplies			2 100 00		4
5	Office Supplies			1 600 00		5
6	Prepaid Insurance			4 800 00		6
7	Store Equipment			104 000 00		7
8	Accumulated Depreciation—Store Equipment				20 000 00	8
9	Office Equipment			80 000 00		9
10	Accumulated Depreciation—Office Equipment				14 000 00	10
11	Accounts Payable				65 000 00	11
12	Mortgage Note Payable (due 5 years)				90 000 00	12
13	Capital Stock				300 000 00	13
14	Retained Earnings				94 750 00	14
15	Dividends			20 000 00		15
16	Sales		517 900 00			16
17	Sales Discounts	6 250 00				17
18	Purchases	266 000 00				18
19	Purchases Discounts		4 200 00			19
20	Purchases Returns and Allowances		6 800 00			20
21	Transportation In	2 600 00				21
22	Advertising Expense	5 000 00				22
23	Sales Salaries Expense	54 300 00				23
24	Office Salaries Expense	27 400 00				24
25	Interest Income		3 600 00			25
26	Interest Expense	9 000 00				26
27	Income Summary	186 000 00	193 000 00			27
28	Store Supplies Expense	2 400 00				28
29	Office Supplies Expense	1 900 00				29
30	Insurance Expense	1 050 00				30
31	Salaries Payable				2 150 00	31
32	Depreciation Expense—Store Equipment	4 000 00				32
33	Depreciation Expense—Office Equipment	2 000 00				33
34	Rent Expense	78 000 00				34
35		645 900 00	725 500 00	665 500 00	585 900 00	35
36	Net Income	79 600 00			79 600 00	36
37		725 500 00	725 500 00	665 500 00	665 500 00	37
38						38

1. *(Cont'd.)*

Required:

(a) Prepare a multi-step income statement for the current fiscal year for J-Pat Fan Corporation using Form A.

(b) Prepare a retained earnings statement using Form B.

(c) Prepare a balance sheet in report form for the J-Pat Fan Corporation using Form C.

(d) Prepare the entries necessary to adjust Merchandise Inventory using the journal form provided on page 53.

(e) Prepare closing entries using the journal provided on page 53.

FORM A

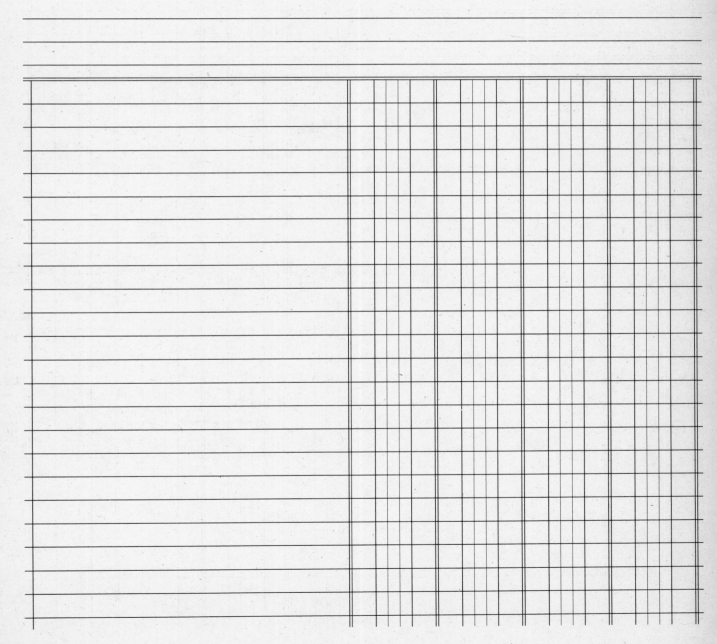

Chapter 5 (Continued)

1. *(Cont'd.)*

FORM A (Cont'd.)

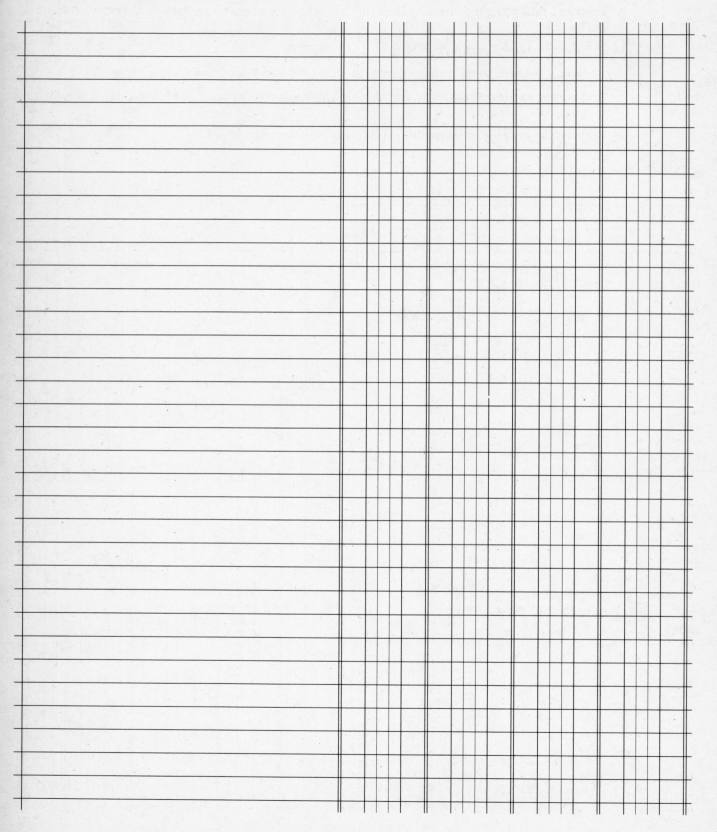

1. *(Cont'd.)*

FORM B

Chapter 5 (Continued)

1. *(Cont'd.)*

FORM C

1. *(Cont'd.)*

JOURNAL

PAGE

	DATE		DESCRIPTION	POST. REF.	DEBIT	CREDIT	
1							1
2							2
3							3
4							4
5							5
6							6
7							7
8							8
9							9
10							10
11							11
12							12
13							13
14							14
15							15
16							16
17							17
18							18
19							19
20							20
21							21
22							22
23							23
24							24
25							25
26							26
27							27
28							28
29							29
30							30
31							31
32							32
33							33
34							34

2. *Combined single-step income and retained earnings statement.*

All of the accounts related to the income statement and retained earnings statement of the Biggie Corporation after adjustments on October 31, the end of the current fiscal year, are presented below.

Advertising Expense	$ 6,000
Depreciation Expense—Office Equipment	5,400
Depreciation Expense—Store Equipment	8,400
Dividends	50,000
Insurance Expense—Administrative	2,850
Insurance Expense—Selling	3,300
Interest Expense	4,820
Interest Income	2,100
Merchandise Inventory, November 1	101,200
Merchandise Inventory, October 31	97,900
Miscellaneous Administrative Expense	610
Miscellaneous Selling Expense	580
Office Salaries Expense	44,600
Office Supplies Expense	1,420
Purchases	347,220
Purchases Discount	2,240
Purchases Returns and Allowances	3,160
Rent Expense	18,000
Retained Earnings, November 1	283,440
Sales Salaries Expense	74,800
Sales	792,400
Sales Returns and Allowances	4,400
Store Supplies Expense	3,860
Taxes Expense	29,200
Utilities Expense	59,480

Prepare a combined single-step income statement and retained earnings statement for the year using Forms A and B respectively on the following pages.

2. *(Cont'd.)*

FORM A

FORM B

3. *Adjusting entries for merchandise inventory; closing entries and retained earnings statement.*

The income summary account for the Freeman Corporation afer the adjusting entries for merchandise inventory and the closing entries have been posted is as follows:

ACCOUNT **Income Summary**   ACCOUNT NO. **313**

DATE		ITEM	POST. REF.	DEBIT	CREDIT	BALANCE DEBIT	BALANCE CREDIT
19-- Dec.	31	Merchandise inventory					
		January 1	41	20 1 4 5 00		20 1 4 5 00	
	31	Merchandise inventory					
		December 31	41		19 3 3 5 00	8 1 0 00	
	31	Revenue, etc.	42		260 4 9 5 00		259 6 8 5 00
	31	Expense, etc.	42	195 9 1 0 00			63 7 7 5 00
	31	Net income	42	63 7 7 5 00			

Dividends paid by the Freeman Corporation for the current year were $20,000. The retained earnings balance on January 1 was $98,000.

(a) Prepare the entries to adjust the merchandise inventory account for the Freeman Corporation.

JOURNAL   PAGE

	DATE		DESCRIPTION	POST. REF.	DEBIT	CREDIT	
1							1
2							2
3							3
4							4
5							5
6							6
7							7
8							8
9							9

3. *(Cont'd.)*

(b) Prepare the closing entries in summary form (revenues as a total and expenses as a total) for the Freeman Corporation.

10						10
11						11
12						12
13						13
14						14
15						15
16						16
17						17
18						18
19						19
20						20
21						21

(c) Prepare a retained earnings statement for the Freeman Corporation for the current year ended December 31.

Chapter 5 (Continued)

4. *Recording reversing entries.*

You are given the following ledger accounts for Leander's Locksmith Shop on December 31, 19--, before adjustments.

ACCOUNT **Salary Expense**

ACCOUNT NO. **720**

DATE		ITEM	POST. REF.	DEBIT	CREDIT	BALANCE	
						DEBIT	CREDIT
19-- Dec.	31	Balance	✔			51 7 0 0 00	

ACCOUNT **Salaries Payable**

ACCOUNT NO. **220**

DATE	ITEM	POST. REF.	DEBIT	CREDIT	BALANCE	
					DEBIT	CREDIT

(a) The weekly pay period for Leander's Locksmith Shop ends on Friday. On Wednesday, December 31, there was $740 in Salaries Accrued. Prepare the adjusting entry to record the accrued salaries, and post to the accounts above.

JOURNAL

PAGE **16**

	DATE	DESCRIPTION	POST. REF.	DEBIT	CREDIT	
1						1
2						2
3						3
4						4
5						5

(b) Prepare the closing entry necessary on December 31, 19--, and post.

6						6
7						7
8						8
9						9
10						10

4. *(Cont'd.)*

(c) Prepare the reversing entry necessary on January 1, 19--, and post.

(d) Record the payment of the weekly payroll on Friday, January 2, 19--, $1,180 and post to the accounts.

(e) Prepare the entry to record the payment of the weekly payroll on Friday, January 2, for $1,180 assuming no reversing entry was made on December 31.

5. *Adjusting and reversing entries.*

(a) From the information given below for the Coppell Wallpaper Shop, prepare the adjusting entries required on December 31, the end of the current fiscal year.

(1) The prepaid advertising account has a $5,400 balance representing the payment on May 1 of the current year for a 12-month period.

JOURNAL PAGE

	DATE	DESCRIPTION	POST. REF.	DEBIT	CREDIT	
1						1
2						2

(2) Store supplies account balance before adjustment, $310; inventory of store supplies on hand December 31, $78.

Chapter 5 (Continued)

5. *(Cont'd.)*

    (3) Equipment was purchased on January 2 of the current year for $26,440 and is to be depreciated equally over an eight-year period. (No salvage value is estimated.)

    (4) Salaries are $7,500 per week for a five-day week ending on Friday. The last payday was Friday, December 27.

    (b) In the general journal below, prepare the necessary reversing entry(ies) for the Coppell Wallpaper Shop on January 1 of the following year.

6. *Correcting entries.*

In each case below, prepare the journal entries required to correct the ledger accounts of the Lexington Company.

(a) A $560 payment for insurance was recorded as a debit to Interest Expense and a credit to Cash.

(b) Advertising expense of $670 was recorded as a debit to Advertising Expense and a credit to Cash for $760.

(c) Cash of $725 received on Accounts Receivable was debited to Cash and credited to Accounts Payable.

JOURNAL

PAGE

	DATE	DESCRIPTION	POST. REF.	DEBIT	CREDIT	
1						1
2						2
3						3
4						4
5						5
6						6
7						7
8						8

7. *Preparing a work sheet for a merchandising business, including financial statements and adjusting and closing entries.*

(a) Using the adjustment data below, complete the work sheet on the following page for Travis Toy Shop.

Merchandise inventory, December 31, 19-- $20,400

Supplies used:

Store supplies.. 610

Office supplies... 320

Insurance expired during year 840

Accrued salaries (to be paid on next regular payday):

Sales salaries 590

Office salaries 420

Accrued taxes.. 410

Depreciation for year:

Building 9,200

Equipment 12,800

Use the following accounts and account numbers:

Income Summary	330	Salaries Payable	212
Store Supplies Expense	613	Taxes Payable	213
Office Supplies Expense......	713	Depreciation Expense........	715
Insurance Expense	714		

Chapter 5 (Continued)

7. *(Cont'd.)*

(a)

Travis Toy Shop
Work Sheet
For Year Ended December 31, 19--

Acct. No.	Account Title	Trial Balance Dr.	Trial Balance Cr.	Adjustments Dr.	Adjustments Cr.	Income Statement Dr.	Income Statement Cr.	Balance Sheet Dr.	Balance Sheet Cr.
111	Cash	16,400							
112	Accounts Receivable	21,600							
113	Mdse. Inventory	37,400							
114	Supplies	2,000							
115	Prepaid Insurance	4,200							
121	Land	95,000							
122	Building	160,000							
123	Accum. Depr.—Building		46,000						
124	Equipment	95,000							
129	Accum. Depr.—Equipment		21,500						
211	Accounts Payable		11,200						
221	Mortgage Payable		75,000						
311	James Travis, Capital		260,850						
312	James Travis, Drawing	12,000							
410	Sales		164,300						
412	Sale Discounts	16,500							
413	Sales Returns & Allow.	24,750							
510	Purchases	82,600							
512	Purchases Discounts		10,900						
513	Purchases Returns & Allow.		16,300						
611	Sales Salaries Expense	20,700							
612	Advertising Expense	420							
619	Misc. Selling Expense	1,400							
711	Office Salaries Expense	13,400							
712	Taxes Expense	480							
719	Misc. Admin. Expense	2,200							
		606,050	606,050						

7. *(Cont'd.)*

    (b) Prepare a multiple-step income statement for Travis Toy Shop from the data on the work sheet prepared.

7. *(Cont'd.)*

(c) Prepare a statement of owner's equity for Travis Toy Shop.

7. *(Cont'd.)*

(d) Prepare a balance sheet for Travis Toy Shop.

7. *(Cont'd.)*

(e) Journalize the adjusting entries from the work sheet prepared for Travis Toy Shop.

JOURNAL

PAGE **23**

	DATE		DESCRIPTION	POST. REF.	DEBIT	CREDIT	
1							1
2							2
3							3
4							4
5							5
6							6
7							7
8							8
9							9
10							10
11							11
12							12
13							13
14							14
15							15
16							16
17							17
18							18
19							19
20							20
21							21
22							22
23							23
24							24
25							25
26							26
27							27
28							28
29							29
30							30
31							31

7. *(Cont'd.)*

(f) Journalize the closing entries for Travis Toy Shop from the work sheet prepared.

JOURNAL

	DATE		DESCRIPTION	POST. REF.	DEBIT	CREDIT	
1							1
2							2
3							3
4							4
5							5
6							6
7							7
8							8
9							9
10							10
11							11
12							12
13							13
14							14
15							15
16							16
17							17
18							18
19							19
20							20
21							21
22							22
23							23
24							24
25							25
26							26
27							27
28							28
29							29
30							30
31							31

7. *(Cont'd.)*

(g) Post the adjusting and closing entries prepared in (e) and (f) to the merchandise inventory, revenue, expense, capital, drawing, and income summary accounts presented below and on pages 69-71.

ACCOUNT **Merchandise Inventory**   ACCOUNT NO. **113**

DATE		ITEM	POST. REF.	DEBIT	CREDIT	BALANCE DEBIT	BALANCE CREDIT
19-- Jan.	1	Balance	✓			3 7 4 0 0 00	

ACCOUNT **James Travis, Capital**   ACCOUNT NO. **311**

DATE		ITEM	POST. REF.	DEBIT	CREDIT	BALANCE DEBIT	BALANCE CREDIT
19-- Dec.	31	Balance	✓				26 0 8 5 0 00

ACCOUNT **James Travis, Drawing**   ACCOUNT NO. **312**

DATE		ITEM	POST. REF.	DEBIT	CREDIT	BALANCE DEBIT	BALANCE CREDIT
19-- Dec.	31	Balance	✓			1 2 0 0 0 00	

ACCOUNT **Income Summary**   ACCOUNT NO. **330**

DATE		ITEM	POST. REF.	DEBIT	CREDIT	BALANCE DEBIT	BALANCE CREDIT

7. *(Cont'd.)*

(g)

ACCOUNT **Sales**   ACCOUNT NO. **410**

DATE		ITEM	POST. REF.	DEBIT	CREDIT	BALANCE	
						DEBIT	CREDIT
19-- Dec.	31	Balance	✓				16 4 3 0 0 00

ACCOUNT **Sales Discounts**   ACCOUNT NO. **412**

DATE		ITEM	POST. REF.	DEBIT	CREDIT	BALANCE	
						DEBIT	CREDIT
19-- Dec.	31	Balance	✓			1 6 5 0 0 00	

ACCOUNT **Sales Returns and Allowances**   ACCOUNT NO. **413**

DATE		ITEM	POST. REF.	DEBIT	CREDIT	BALANCE	
						DEBIT	CREDIT
19-- Dec.	31	Balance	✓			2 4 7 5 0 00	

ACCOUNT **Purchases**   ACCOUNT NO. **510**

DATE		ITEM	POST. REF.	DEBIT	CREDIT	BALANCE	
						DEBIT	CREDIT
19-- Dec.	31	Balance	✓			8 2 6 0 0 00	

ACCOUNT **Purchases Discounts**   ACCOUNT NO. **512**

DATE		ITEM	POST. REF.	DEBIT	CREDIT	BALANCE	
						DEBIT	CREDIT
19-- Dec.	31	Balance	✓				1 0 9 0 0 00

ACCOUNT **Purchases Returns and Allowances**   ACCOUNT NO. **513**

DATE		ITEM	POST. REF.	DEBIT	CREDIT	BALANCE	
						DEBIT	CREDIT
19-- Dec.	31	Balance	✓				1 6 3 0 0 00

7. *(Cont'd.)*

(g)

ACCOUNT **Sales Salaries Expense**   ACCOUNT NO. **611**

DATE		ITEM	POST. REF.	DEBIT	CREDIT	BALANCE	
						DEBIT	CREDIT
19-- Dec.	31	Balance	✔			2 0 7 0 0 00	

ACCOUNT **Advertising Expense**   ACCOUNT NO. **612**

DATE		ITEM	POST. REF.	DEBIT	CREDIT	BALANCE	
						DEBIT	CREDIT
19-- Dec.	31	Balance	✔			4 2 0 00	

ACCOUNT **Store Supplies Expense**   ACCOUNT NO. **613**

DATE		ITEM	POST. REF.	DEBIT	CREDIT	BALANCE	
						DEBIT	CREDIT

ACCOUNT **Miscellaneous Selling Expense**   ACCOUNT NO. **619**

DATE		ITEM	POST. REF.	DEBIT	CREDIT	BALANCE	
						DEBIT	CREDIT
19-- Dec.	31	Balance	✔			1 4 0 0 00	

ACCOUNT **Office Salaries Expense**   ACCOUNT NO. **711**

DATE		ITEM	POST. REF.	DEBIT	CREDIT	BALANCE	
						DEBIT	CREDIT
19-- Dec.	31	Balance	✔			1 3 4 0 0 00	

7. *(Cont'd.)*

(g)

ACCOUNT **Taxes Expense**   ACCOUNT NO. **712**

DATE		ITEM	POST. REF.	DEBIT	CREDIT	BALANCE	
						DEBIT	CREDIT
19-- Dec.	31	Balance	✓			4 8 0 00	

ACCOUNT **Office Supplies Expense**   ACCOUNT NO. **713**

DATE		ITEM	POST. REF.	DEBIT	CREDIT	BALANCE	
						DEBIT	CREDIT

ACCOUNT **Insurance Expense**   ACCOUNT NO. **714**

DATE		ITEM	POST. REF.	DEBIT	CREDIT	BALANCE	
						DEBIT	CREDIT

ACCOUNT **Depreciation Expense**   ACCOUNT NO. **715**

DATE		ITEM	POST. REF.	DEBIT	CREDIT	BALANCE	
						DEBIT	CREDIT

ACCOUNT **Miscellaneous Administrative Expense**   ACCOUNT NO. **719**

DATE		ITEM	POST. REF.	DEBIT	CREDIT	BALANCE	
						DEBIT	CREDIT
19-- Dec.	31	Balance	✓			2 2 0 0 00	

Notes from lecture and study:

1. *Internal control.*

   The following statements relate to a system of internal control. Indicate whether each statement is true or false by placing a check mark in the appropriate column.

	True	False
(a) Internal accounting controls consist of only procedures and records that are primarily concerned with the reliability of financial records and reports.		
(b) Internal administrative controls consist of procedures and records that assist management in achieving business objectives.		
(c) Details of a system of internal control will depend on the size and type of business.		
(d) Key employees should be discouraged from taking vacations because of the difficulty of covering their jobs during their absence.		
(e) Rotating clerical personnel periodically from job to job is not helpful in disclosing irregularities that may have occurred.		
(f) A weakness in the system of "checks and balances" provided by distributing responsibility among various departments is the duplication of effort.		
(g) In proper accounting systems, the person ordering merchandise should not verify the receipt of the goods and pay the supplier.		
(h) Responsibility for maintaining the accounting records should be separated from the custody of the assets.		
(i) A good system of internal control will include a periodic review and evaluation by management.		
(j) One of the principal devices for maintaining control over cash is the bank statement.		

Chapter 6 (Continued)

2. *Purchases journal and postings.*

(a) Record the following invoices in the purchases journal below for Betsy's Bath Shop, and post to the ledger on the following page.

July 2. Katz Manufacturing, $840 for merchandise.

10. Laurie Supply Company, $2,080 (for office supplies, $240; store supplies, $210; and merchandise, $1,630).

16. Hee Supplies, $630 (for office supplies, $250; store supplies, $380).

19. Laurie Supply Company, $3,280 for office equipment.

25. Katz Manufacturing, $3,660 for merchandise.

30. Hee Supplies, $2,320 (for office supplies, $150; store supplies, $260; and store equipment, $1,910).

PURCHASES JOURNAL

DATE	ACCOUNT CREDITED	POST. REF.	ACCOUNTS PAYABLE CR.	PURCHASES DR.	STORE SUPPLIES DR.	OFFICE SUPPLIES DR.	SUNDRY ACCOUNTS DR.		
							ACCOUNT	POST. REF.	AMOUNT

2. *(Cont'd.)*

Store Supplies	(16)

Office Equipment	(27)

Office Supplies	(17)

Accounts Payable	(31)

Store Equipment	(26)

Purchases	(51)

NAME   **Hee Supplies**

ADDRESS   **2120 South Fifth Street**

DATE	ITEM	POST. REF.	DEBIT	CREDIT	BALANCE

NAME   **Katz Manufacturing**

ADDRESS   **126 Nottingham Road**

DATE	ITEM	POST. REF.	DEBIT	CREDIT	BALANCE

NAME   **Laurie Supply Company**

ADDRESS   **28 USC Drive**

DATE	ITEM	POST. REF.	DEBIT	CREDIT	BALANCE

2. *(Cont'd.)*

(b) What is the total of the accounts payable subsidiary ledger on July 31? (Prepare a schedule of accounts.)

_____

_____

_____

_____

3. *Cash payments journal and postings.*

Record the following payments for Camp Wholesalers for the month of March in the cash payments journal provided, and post to the subsidiary ledger and general ledger.

March 1. Paid rent expense for September, $2,000. (Check No. 620)
　　　　 4. Paid Amy Company $1,649, representing balance owed less 3% discount. (Check No. 621)
　　　　 7. Purchased office supplies for cash, $610. (Check No. 622)
　　　 16. Paid Gibson Supplies $640 for cash purchase of merchandise. (Check No. 623)
　　　 22. Paid Rose Wholesalers $2,200 on invoice with n/30 billing. (Check No. 624)
　　　 26. Paid cash customer $75 for merchandise returned. (Check No. 625)
　　　 29. Annie Camp withdrew $1,150 for personal use. (Check No. 626)
　　　 30. Paid monthly utility bill, $1,440. (Check No. 627)
　　　 30. Paid Blanton Supply Company $1,406, representing balance owed less 5% discount. (Check No. 628)

CASH PAYMENTS JOURNAL
PAGE **16**

	DATE	CK. NO.	ACCOUNT DEBITED	POST. REF.	SUNDRY ACCOUNTS DR.	ACCOUNTS PAYABLE DR.	PURCHASES DISCOUNT CR.	CASH CR.	
1									1
2									2
3									3
4									4
5									5
6									6
7									7
8									8
9									9
10									10
11									11
12									12
13									13
14									14
15									15
16									16

3. *(Cont'd.)*

ACCOUNTS PAYABLE LEDGER

NAME   **Amy Company**

ADDRESS   **2371 Warrensville Road**

DATE		ITEM	POST. REF.	DEBIT	CREDIT	BALANCE
19-- Mar.	1	Balance	✓			1 7 0 0 00

NAME   **Rose Wholesalers**

ADDRESS   **1056 Park Lane**

DATE		ITEM	POST. REF.	DEBIT	CREDIT	BALANCE
19-- Mar.	1	Balance	✓			2 2 0 0 00

NAME   **Blanton Supply Company**

ADDRESS   **7771 Montgomery Road**

DATE		ITEM	POST. REF.	DEBIT	CREDIT	BALANCE
19-- Mar.	1	Balance	✓			1 4 8 0 00

GENERAL LEDGER

(Note: You do not have all of the accounts for the general ledger; consequently, the ledger will not balance.)

ACCOUNT   **Cash**   ACCOUNT NO. **11**

DATE		ITEM	POST. REF.	DEBIT	CREDIT	BALANCE	
						DEBIT	CREDIT
19-- Mar.	1	Balance				12 3 0 0 00	

ACCOUNT   **Accounts Receivable**   ACCOUNT NO. **12**

DATE		ITEM	POST. REF.	DEBIT	CREDIT	BALANCE	
						DEBIT	CREDIT
19-- Mar.	1	Balance	✓			4 1 5 0 00	
	31		S11	9 6 0 0 00		13 7 5 0 00	

3. *(Cont'd.)*

ACCOUNT **Office Supplies**   ACCOUNT NO. **15**

DATE		ITEM	POST. REF.	DEBIT	CREDIT	BALANCE DEBIT	BALANCE CREDIT
19-- Mar.	1	Balance	✔			2 0 7 00	

ACCOUNT **Accounts Payable**   ACCOUNT NO. **31**

DATE		ITEM	POST. REF.	DEBIT	CREDIT	BALANCE DEBIT	BALANCE CREDIT
19-- Mar.	1	Balance	✔				5 3 8 0 00
	31		P14		4 3 4 0 00		9 7 2 0 00

ACCOUNT **Annie Camp, Capital**   ACCOUNT NO. **41**

DATE		ITEM	POST. REF.	DEBIT	CREDIT	BALANCE DEBIT	BALANCE CREDIT
19-- Mar.	1	Balance	✔				9 5 1 0 00

ACCOUNT **Annie Camp, Drawing**   ACCOUNT NO. **42**

DATE		ITEM	POST. REF.	DEBIT	CREDIT	BALANCE DEBIT	BALANCE CREDIT

ACCOUNT **Sales**   ACCOUNT NO. **51**

DATE		ITEM	POST. REF.	DEBIT	CREDIT	BALANCE DEBIT	BALANCE CREDIT
19-- Mar.	31		S11		9 6 0 0 00		9 6 0 0 00

ACCOUNT **Sales Returns and Allowances**   ACCOUNT NO. **52**

DATE		ITEM	POST. REF.	DEBIT	CREDIT	BALANCE DEBIT	BALANCE CREDIT

3. *(Cont'd.)*

ACCOUNT **Sales Discounts**   ACCOUNT NO. **53**

DATE		ITEM	POST. REF.	DEBIT	CREDIT	BALANCE	
						DEBIT	CREDIT

ACCOUNT **Purchases**   ACCOUNT NO. **61**

DATE		ITEM	POST. REF.	DEBIT	CREDIT	BALANCE	
						DEBIT	CREDIT
19-- Mar.	31		P14	4 3 4 0 00		4 3 4 0 00	

ACCOUNT **Purchases Discounts**   ACCOUNT NO. **63**

DATE		ITEM	POST. REF.	DEBIT	CREDIT	BALANCE	
						DEBIT	CREDIT

ACCOUNT **Rent Expense**   ACCOUNT NO. **73**

DATE		ITEM	POST. REF.	DEBIT	CREDIT	BALANCE	
						DEBIT	CREDIT

ACCOUNT **Utilities Expense**   ACCOUNT NO. **75**

DATE		ITEM	POST. REF.	DEBIT	CREDIT	BALANCE	
						DEBIT	CREDIT

Chapter 6 (Continued)

4. *Sales journal and postings.*

(a) Record the following charge sales tickets in the sales journal of Blankenship's Medical Supplies, and post all transactions for the month of April.

April 18 to Cartright Medical Clinic, $680; invoice 921.
April 20 to Shadle Medical Center, $570; invoice 922.
April 24 to Medical Arts, $390; invoice 923.
April 28 to Community Hospital, $470; invoice 924.

Blankenship's Medical Supplies
2609 Picadilly
Tulsa, OK 74101

Apr. 18   No.   921

To: Cartwright Medical Clinic
Santa Barbara, CA 93102

| 10 | Item A17 | 68.00 | 680.00 |

SALES JOURNAL

PAGE 20

DATE		INVOICE NO.	ACCOUNT DEBITED	POST. REF.	ACCTS. REC. DR. SALES CR.
Apr.	4	917	Cartright Medical Clinic	✔	3 3 0 00
	9	918	Medical Arts	✔	5 4 0 00
	12	919	Community Hospital	✔	9 3 0 00
	14	920	Shadle Medical Center	✔	7 0 0 00

ACCOUNTS RECEIVABLE LEDGER

NAME   **Cartright Medical Clinic**

ADDRESS   **1328 Dartmouth Circle**

DATE	ITEM	POST. REF.	DEBIT	CREDIT	BALANCE

NAME   **Community Hospital**

ADDRESS   **4308 Teasley Road**

DATE	ITEM	POST. REF.	DEBIT	CREDIT	BALANCE

4. *(Cont'd.)*

(a)

NAME **Medical Arts**

ADDRESS **1413 Panhandle Drive**

DATE	ITEM	POST. REF.	DEBIT	CREDIT	BALANCE

NAME **Shadle Medical Center**

ADDRESS **1400 Malone Street**

DATE	ITEM	POST. REF.	DEBIT	CREDIT	BALANCE

GENERAL LEDGER

ACCOUNT **Accounts Receivable**   ACCOUNT NO. **12**

DATE	ITEM	POST. REF.	DEBIT	CREDIT	BALANCE DEBIT	BALANCE CREDIT

ACCOUNT **Sales**   ACCOUNT NO. **41**

DATE	ITEM	POST. REF.	DEBIT	CREDIT	BALANCE DEBIT	BALANCE CREDIT

(b) What is the total of the accounts receivable subsidiary ledger for Blankenship's Medical Supplies on April 30? (Prepare a schedule of accounts.)

_____

_____

_____

_____

_____

_____

_____

Chapter 6 (Continued)

5. *Cash receipts journal and postings.*

(a) Record the following transactions in the cash receipts journal of Camp Wholesalers.

March 3. Received $1,029 from Egypt Company as payment of March 1 balance, less 2% discount.

9. Received $1,666 from Whirlwinds in payment of account on March 1, less 2% discount.

11. Cash sales, $2,510.

19. Received $2,000 as an additional investment from Annie Camp, the proprietor.

23. Sold $75 of office supplies (not a merchandise item) to MacArthur for cash as a convenience to them.

28. Received $1,400 from JHS Co. in payment of March 1 balance.

31. Cash sales $2,240.

CASH RECEIPTS JOURNAL

	DATE		ACCOUNT CREDITED	POST. REF.	SUNDRY ACCOUNTS CR.	SALES CR.	ACCOUNTS REC. CR.	SALES DISCOUNT DR.	CASH DR.	
1										1
2										2
3										3
4										4
5										5
6										6
7										7
8										8
9										9
10										10
11										11
12										12
13										13

(b) Post the cash receipts journal to the subsidiary ledger below and the general ledger on the following page.

ACCOUNTS RECEIVABLE LEDGER

NAME **Egypt Company**

ADDRESS **1607 Castle Lane**

DATE		ITEM	POST. REF.	DEBIT	CREDIT	BALANCE
19-- Mar.	1	Balance	✓			1 0 5 0 00
	6		S11	1 3 5 0 00		2 4 0 0 00
	17		S11	6 7 0 00		3 0 7 0 00

5. *(Cont'd.)*

(b)

NAME   JHS Co.

ADDRESS   1001 Gee Street

DATE		ITEM	POST. REF.	DEBIT	CREDIT	BALANCE
19-- Mar.	1	Balance	✔			1 4 0 0 00
	10		S11	2 7 9 0 00		4 1 9 0 00
	28		S11	7 0 0 00		4 8 9 0 00

NAME   **Whirlwinds**

ADDRESS   **6210 Highland Drive**

DATE		ITEM	POST. REF.	DEBIT	CREDIT	BALANCE
19-- Mar.	1	Balance	✔			1 7 0 0 00
	2		S11	1 6 3 0 00		3 3 3 0 00
	22		S11	2 4 6 0 00		5 7 9 0 00

GENERAL LEDGER

ACCOUNT   **Cash**   ACCOUNT NO. **11**

DATE		ITEM	POST. REF.	DEBIT	CREDIT	BALANCE DEBIT	BALANCE CREDIT
19-- Mar.	1	Balance	✔			12 3 0 0 00	
	31		CP16		11 1 7 0 00	1 1 3 0 00	

ACCOUNT   **Accounts Receivable**   ACCOUNT NO. **12**

DATE		ITEM	POST. REF.	DEBIT	CREDIT	BALANCE DEBIT	BALANCE CREDIT
19-- Mar.	1	Balance	✔			4 1 5 0 00	
	31		S11	9 6 0 0 00		13 7 5 0 00	

5. *(Cont'd.)*

(b)

ACCOUNT **Office Supplies**   ACCOUNT NO. **15**

DATE		ITEM	POST. REF.	DEBIT	CREDIT	BALANCE	
						DEBIT	CREDIT
19-- Mar.	1	Balance	✓			2 0 7 00	
	7		CP16	6 1 0 00		8 1 7 00	

ACCOUNT **Accounts Payable**   ACCOUNT NO. **31**

DATE		ITEM	POST. REF.	DEBIT	CREDIT	BALANCE	
						DEBIT	CREDIT
19-- Mar.	1	Balance	✓				5 3 8 0 00
	31		P14		4 3 4 0 00		9 7 2 0 00
	31		CP16	5 3 8 0 00			4 3 4 0 00

ACCOUNT **Annie Camp, Capital**   ACCOUNT NO. **41**

DATE		ITEM	POST. REF.	DEBIT	CREDIT	BALANCE	
						DEBIT	CREDIT
19-- Mar.	1	Balance	✓				9 5 1 0 00

ACCOUNT **Annie Camp, Drawing**   ACCOUNT NO. **42**

DATE		ITEM	POST. REF.	DEBIT	CREDIT	BALANCE	
						DEBIT	CREDIT
19-- Mar.	31		CP16	1 1 5 0 00		1 1 5 0 00	

ACCOUNT **Sales**   ACCOUNT NO. **51**

DATE		ITEM	POST. REF.	DEBIT	CREDIT	BALANCE	
						DEBIT	CREDIT
19-- Mar.	31		S11		9 6 0 0 00		9 6 0 0 00

5. *(Cont'd.)*

(b)

ACCOUNT **Sales Returns and Allowances**　　　　　　　　　　　　ACCOUNT NO. **52**

DATE		ITEM	POST. REF.	DEBIT	CREDIT	BALANCE	
						DEBIT	CREDIT
19-- Mar.	26		CP16	7 5 00		7 5 00	

ACCOUNT **Sales Discounts**　　　　　　　　　　　　ACCOUNT NO. **53**

DATE	ITEM	POST. REF.	DEBIT	CREDIT	BALANCE	
					DEBIT	CREDIT

ACCOUNT **Purchases**　　　　　　　　　　　　ACCOUNT NO. **61**

DATE		ITEM	POST. REF.	DEBIT	CREDIT	BALANCE	
						DEBIT	CREDIT
19-- Mar.	16		CP16	6 4 0 00		6 4 0 00	
	31		P14	4 3 4 0 00		4 9 8 0 00	

ACCOUNT **Purchases Discounts**　　　　　　　　　　　　ACCOUNT NO. **63**

DATE		ITEM	POST. REF.	DEBIT	CREDIT	BALANCE	
						DEBIT	CREDIT
19-- Mar.	31		CP16		1 2 5 00		1 2 5 00

ACCOUNT **Rent Expense**　　　　　　　　　　　　ACCOUNT NO. **73**

DATE		ITEM	POST. REF.	DEBIT	CREDIT	BALANCE	
						DEBIT	CREDIT
19-- Mar.	1		CP16	2 0 0 0 00		2 0 0 0 00	

ACCOUNT **Utilities Expense**　　　　　　　　　　　　ACCOUNT NO. **75**

DATE		ITEM	POST. REF.	DEBIT	CREDIT	BALANCE	
						DEBIT	CREDIT
19-- Mar.	31		CP16	1 4 4 0 00		1 4 4 0 00	

6. *Recording memorandums and correcting errors.*

Record the following transactions in the general journal provided. Assume that all incorrect entries have been posted and that the corrections are recorded in the same period in which the error occurred.

June 1. Issued a credit memorandum to Calgary Company for return of merchandise sold on account on May 22, $725.

  3. Discovered that a check for $510 received from Lakeman Company as payment on account was recorded as a cash sale.

  6. Discovered that transportation costs of $82 on purchase of merchandise had been debited to Purchases.

  8. Received a credit memorandum for return of copy machine (Office Equipment) purchased on account from Cheateau Office Equipment Co. on June 2, $1,040.

  11. Issued a debit memorandum for return of merchandise purchased on account from Copas Industries on June 6, $660.

  15. A cash sale to Don Graywolf in the amount of $315 was recorded as a sale on account.

  19. Issued a credit memorandum to Hector Lopez for allowance for defective merchandise sold on account on June 9, $380.

  22. Discovered that a $605 cash purchase of merchandise from PAS Corporation had been recorded as a purchase on account.

6. *(Cont'd.)*

JOURNAL

PAGE

	DATE	DESCRIPTION	POST. REF.	DEBIT	CREDIT	
1						1
2						2
3						3
4						4
5						5
6						6
7						7
8						8
9						9
10						10
11						11
12						12
13						13
14						14
15						15
16						16
17						17
18						18
19						19
20						20
21						21
22						22
23						23
24						24
25						25
26						26
27						27
28						28
29						29
30						30
31						31
32						32

7. *Review of special journals.*

Below are listed several books of original entry, each of which is designated by one or two letters. Indicate the journal in which each transaction can be recorded most conveniently by printing the letter or letters corresponding to that journal in Column A. Also indicate whether an account in the accounts receivable or accounts payable subsidiary ledgers will be affected by each transaction by placing an AR or AP in Column B.

CP Cash Payments	G General Journal	S Sales Journal
CR Cash Receipts	P Purchases Journal	

	Column A Journal Recorded	Column B Subsidiary Affected
(a) Returned for credit merchandise purchased on account.		
(b) Made a correcting entry debiting office supplies and crediting office equipment.		
(c) Paid insurance premiums for two years in advance.		
(d) Sold merchandise for cash.		
(e) Sold store supplies on account at cost.		
(f) Borrowed money from bank on 90-day note payable.		
(g) Purchased merchandise for cash.		
(h) Received a check in payment of note receivable.		
(i) Issued credit memo for damaged merchandise.		
(j) Received payment from customer on account.		
(k) Paid creditor for merchandise purchased on account.		
(l) Closed drawing account.		
(m) Paid for store supplies purchased on account.		
(n) Sold merchandise on account.		
(o) Paid cash to customer for merchandise returned.		
(p) Owner invested additional cash in business.		
(q) Purchased merchandise on account.		
(r) Paid monthly rent.		
(s) Adjusting entry for depreciation of equipment.		
(t) Recorded cash sales for the week.		

Notes from lecture and study:

_____

_____

_____

_____

_____

_____

_____

_____

_____

_____

_____

_____

_____

_____

_____

_____

_____

_____

_____

_____

_____

_____

_____

Chapter 7 (Continued)

1. *Bank reconciliation—basic.*

   (a) From the following information, prepare a bank reconciliation for the Hancock Company on April 30, 19--.

Customers' checks returned NSF	$ 84
Balance per bank statement, April 30.........................	1,973
Checks outstanding	580
Customer's note collected by bank, not recorded on books	390
Interest collected on above note	30
Bank service charges for April...............................	26
Check No. 803 for rent expense recorded in cash payments journal as $860 but paid by the bank in the correct amount of	680
Deposits in transit	410
Balance per checkbook, April 30.............................	1,313

1. *(Cont'd.)*

(b) Prepare the entries, in general journal form, to correct the cash account for the Hancock Company.

JOURNAL

	DATE		DESCRIPTION	POST. REF.	DEBIT	CREDIT	
1							1
2							2
3							3
4							4
5							5
6							6
7							7
8							8
9							9
10							10
11							11
12							12

2. *Bank reconciliation—detail.*

Following is the information taken from the checkbook stubs of Chang Home Alarm Company for the month of October of the current year.

Date	Check No.	Amount	Deposit	Balance
Oct. 1				$ 863.00
1	537	$ 27.00		836.00
2	538	41.50	$210.00	1,004.50
4	539	32.00		972.50
6	540	20.00		952.50
9	541	50.00		902.50
10	542	83.90	200.00	1,018.60
12	543	62.00		956.60
14	544	15.00		941.60
15	545	27.00		914.60
18	546	39.00		875.60
18	547	43.00	185.00	1,017.60
21	548	VOID		1,017.60
21	549	100.00		917.60
26	550	22.00		895.60
30	551	37.50		858.10
31	552	19.80	260.00	1,098.30

Chang's bank statement is presented at the top of page 92. Checks that were outstanding on the September bank reconciliation are as follows: Check No. 510, $20; Check No. 513, $65; Check No. 533, $130.

2. *(Cont'd.)*

Pacific National Bank

STATEMENT
OF
ACCOUNT

Chang Home Alarm Company
1991 Colorado Avenue
Seattle, WA 98199-6742

ACCOUNT NUMBER
141-53566

10/31/--
DATE OF STATEMENT

BALANCE FROM PREVIOUS STATEMENT	NUMBER OF DEBITS	AMOUNT OF CHECKS AND DEBITS	NUMBER OF CREDITS	AMOUNT OF DEPOSITS AND CREDITS	SERVICE CHARGE	STATEMENT BALANCE
1,078.00	15	718.40	4	705.00	17.00	1,047.60

DATE	CHECKS DEBITS	CHECKS DEBITS	DEPOSITS CREDITS	BALANCE
10/2	20.00	65.00		993.00
10/4	27.00		210.00	1,176.00
10/5	130.00	32.00		1,014.00
10/8	41.50	20.00	MS 110.00	1,062.50
10/11	50.00	83.90	200.00	1,128.60
10/16	27.00			1,101.60
10/19	39.00	62.00		1,000.60
10/20	43.00		185.00	1,142.60
10/27	22.00			1,120.60
10/31	17.00SC	56.00NSF		1,047.60

PLEASE EXAMINE AT ONCE. IF NO ERROR IS REPORTED WITHIN 10 DAYS THE ACCOUNT WILL BE CONSIDERED CORRECT AND VOUCHERS GENUINE. REFER ANY DISCREPANCY OR ERROR TO OUR BOOKKEEPING DEPT.

EC-ERROR CORRECTION   MS-MISCELLANEOUS   SC-SERVICE CHARGE
NSF-NOT SUFFICIENT FUNDS   OD-OVERDRAFT

Checks returned by the bank with the October statement are rearranged in numerical sequence below.

Check No.	Amount	Check No.	Amount
510	$ 20.00	541	$50.00
513	65.00	542	83.90
533	130.00	543	62.00
537	27.00	545	27.00
538	41.50	546	39.00
539	32.00	547	43.00
540	20.00	550	22.00

The $110 collected by the bank was on a note receivable from a customer, Carla Thompson. The note was non-interest bearing. The $56 NSF check was given to Chang by Lowell Chrisco as payment on his account and has been deposited in September.

(a) Prepare a bank reconciliation for Chang Home Alarm Company for the month of October using the ruled paper provided on page 93.

(b) Prepare any entries required to correct the cash account using the two-column journal paper.

2. *(Cont'd.)*

JOURNAL

	DATE	DESCRIPTION	POST. REF.	DEBIT	CREDIT	
1						1
2						2
3						3
4						4
5						5
6						6
7						7
8						8
9						9
10						10
11						11
12						12

Chapter 7 (Continued)

3. *Recording in a voucher register.*

Record the following transactions for the Steward Co. for the month of May using the voucher register and the check register. The bank balance of $3,130 is given. Deposits throughout the month are as shown in the deposits column of the check register.

May   1. Purchased merchandise from Woods Company for $1,460; terms 2/10, n/30; Voucher No. 721.
        2. Purchased store supplies $215 and office supplies $138 from Dee Sales Co.; Voucher No. 722.
        3. Prepared Voucher No. 723 to Kay Realty, $1,100 for monthly rent.
        3. Paid Voucher No. 723; Check No. 807.
        4. Prepared Voucher No. 724 for $100 to establish petty cash fund.
        4. Paid Voucher No. 724; Check No. 808.
        8. Purchased store supplies $185 and merchandise $1,345 from Wilhoite Co.; terms n/30; Voucher No. 725.
     11. Paid Woods Company for Voucher No. 721, less discount; Check No. 809.
     13. Purchased office equipment $900 and office supplies $120 from Dan's; terms n/30; Voucher No. 726.
     14. Paid advertising expense to DFW Agency, $300; Voucher No. 727; Check No. 810.
     16. Paid Voucher No. 722 for $353; Check No. 811.
     19. Purchased merchandise from Woods Company for $700; terms 2/10, n/30; Voucher No. 728.
     25. Paid Voucher No. 725 to Wilhoite Co., $1,530; Check No. 812.
     27. Purchased merchandise from Torrez Co. for cash, $300; Voucher No. 729; Check No. 813.
     28. Paid Voucher No. 728, less discount; Check No. 814.
     30. Prepared Voucher No. 730 to replenish petty cash in the amount of $73 as follows: store supplies, $29; office supplies, $17; miscellaneous, $27; Check No. 815.

VOUCHER REGISTER

DATE	VOU. NO.	PAYEE	PAID DATE	CK. NO.	ACCOUNTS PAYABLE CR.

3. *(Cont'd.)*

CHECK REGISTER

DATE	CK. NO.	PAYEE	VOU. NO.	ACCOUNTS PAYABLE DR.	PURCHASES DISCOUNT CR.	CASH IN BANK CR.	BANK	
							DEPOSITS	BALANCE
								3130 00
							1450 00	
							1240 00	
							605 00	
							760 00	

VOUCHER REGISTER

PAGE

	PURCHASES DR.	STORE SUPPLIES DR.	OFFICE SUPPLIES DR.	SUNDRY ACCOUNTS DR.			
				ACCOUNT	POST. REF.	AMOUNT	
1							1
2							2
3							3
4							4
5							5
6							6
7							7
8							8
9							9
10							10
11							11
12							12
13							13
14							14

Chapter 7 (Continued)

4. *Recording purchases discounts.*

On July 6, the Valdez Company purchases merchandise with an invoice price of $11,800 subject to terms of 3/10, n/30. Prepare the entries, in general journal form, to record the following transactions.

(a) July 6. To purchase the merchandise (assuming all invoices are recorded at the invoice price).

JOURNAL PAGE

	DATE	DESCRIPTION	POST. REF.	DEBIT	CREDIT	
1						1
2						2

July 15. To pay the invoice within the discount period.

3						3
4						4
5						5

July 23. To pay the invoice after the discount period has expired (assuming invoice was not paid July 15).

6						6
7						7

(b) July 6. To purchase the merchandise (assuming invoices are recorded at their net price after deducting allowable discount).

8						8
9						9

July 15. To pay the invoice within the discount period.

10						10
11						11

July 23. To pay the invoice after the discount period has expired (assuming invoice was not paid July 15).

12						12
13						13
14						14

5. *Petty cash fund.*

Prepare, in general journal form, the following entries to record petty cash transactions for Jack Baker Florist.

Nov. 2. Prepare Voucher No. 381 for $120 to establish a petty cash fund.

JOURNAL   PAGE

	DATE	DESCRIPTION	POST. REF.	DEBIT	CREDIT	
1						1
2						2

Nov. 2. Issued Check No. 431 in payment of Voucher No. 381.

Nov. 30. Prepared Voucher No. 402 for $84.30 to replenish the fund. A summary of petty cash receipts is given: postage (miscellaneous expense), $34.40; office supplies, $27.60; cleaning supplies, $22.30.

Nov. 30. Issued Check No. 449 in payment of Voucher No. 402.

Nov. 30. Prepared Voucher No. 407 for $30 to increase the petty cash fund to $150.

Nov. 30. Issued Check No. 454 in payment of Voucher No. 407.

Chapter 8   RECEIVABLES AND TEMPORARY INVESTMENTS

Notes from lecture and study:

1. *Issuing and receiving a promissory note.*

On May 13, 1990, Jim George issues a 90-day, 10% note to the Tinker Realty Company in payment of his account in the amount of $6,000. The note is payable at First National Bank.

(a) Complete the following note for George; it will be Number 51.

```
$ _____          DATE _____ 19 ____

_____ AFTER DATE _____ PROMISE TO PAY TO

THE ORDER OF _____

_____ DOLLARS

PAYABLE AT _____

WITH INTEREST AT _____

NO. _____ DUE _____    _____
```

(b) From the completed note answer the following questions:

(1) Who is the maker? _____

(2) Who is the payee? _____

(3) What is the due date of the note? _____

(4) How much interest will be paid at maturity? _____

(c) Record the journal entry on the books of the Tinker Realty Company to record the issuance of the note.

JOURNAL   PAGE

	DATE	DESCRIPTION	POST. REF.	DEBIT	CREDIT	
1						1
2						2

(d) Record the receipt of payment on the books of the Tinker Realty Company on August 11.

3						3
4						4
5						5

2. *Computing interest and due date.*

Lozano Equipment Company received the following notes from its customers:

(a) Determine the due date and the amount of interest due on each note at maturity.

	Date	Term	Interest Rate	Face Amount	Due Date	Interest Due
(1)	Aug. 5	60 days	10%	$4,200	_____	_____
(2)	Aug. 17	120 days	none	1,600	_____	_____
(3)	Aug. 29	6 months	12%	850	_____	_____
(4)	Sept. 11	90 days	9%	3,200	_____	_____
(5)	Sept. 22	3 months	12%	8,000	_____	_____

(b) Assuming Note 2 was discounted on September 16 at the rate of 10% and that Note 4 was discounted on November 10 at the rate of 12%, determine the following for each:

Note	Maturity Value	Discount Period	Amt. of Discount	Proceeds
2	_____	_____	_____	_____
4	_____	_____	_____	_____

_____

_____

_____

_____

_____

_____

_____

(c) Prepare the entries, in general journal form, to record the discounting of Notes 2 and 4 on the books of Lozano Equipment Company.

JOURNAL

PAGE

	DATE	DESCRIPTION	POST. REF.	DEBIT	CREDIT	
1						1
2						2
3						3
4						4
5						5
6						6
7						7

3. *Notes receivable cycle—discounting, dishonoring.*

Record the following transactions, in general journal form, on the books of the Hoxie Company during the current year.

June 4. Sold merchandise to Skip Mooney on account, $5,600.

JOURNAL

PAGE

	DATE	DESCRIPTION	POST. REF.	DEBIT	CREDIT	
1						1
2						2

July 6. Received a $5,600, 90-day, 10% note from Mooney in payment of his account.

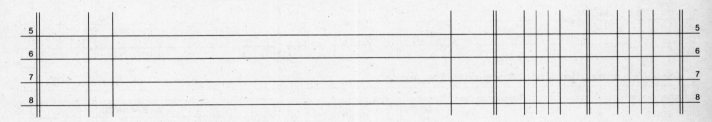

Aug. 5. Discounted Mooney's note at the bank at 12%.

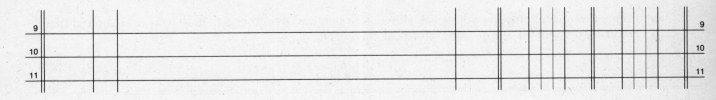

Oct. 3. Bank notifies the Hoxie Company that Mooney has dishonored his note. The Hoxie Company pays the bank the amount due plus a $56 service charge.

Dec. 2. Received the amount due on the dishonored note plus 12% interest on the total owed since the due date.

4. *Accounts receivable accounts and entries.*

The following accounts receivable and sales accounts are for the Coda Chemical Company, December 31, 1990, the end of the first year of operation before adjustments.

ACCOUNT **Accounts Receivable**   ACCOUNT NO. **112**

DATE		ITEM	POST. REF.	DEBIT	CREDIT	BALANCE	
						DEBIT	CREDIT
1990 Dec.	31	Balance				46 7 0 0 00	

ACCOUNT **Allowance for Doubtful Accounts**   ACCOUNT NO. **112.1**

DATE		ITEM	POST. REF.	DEBIT	CREDIT	BALANCE	
						DEBIT	CREDIT

ACCOUNT **Sales**   ACCOUNT NO. **511**

DATE		ITEM	POST. REF.	DEBIT	CREDIT	BALANCE	
						DEBIT	CREDIT
1990 Dec.	31	Balance					188 4 0 0 00

ACCOUNT **Uncollectible Accounts Expense**   ACCOUNT NO. **651**

DATE		ITEM	POST. REF.	DEBIT	CREDIT	BALANCE	
						DEBIT	CREDIT

(a) Prepare a journal entry to adjust the above accounts on December 31, 1990, if it is estimated that credit losses will be 2% of sales, and post the entry.

JOURNAL   PAGE

	DATE		DESCRIPTION	POST. REF.	DEBIT	CREDIT	
1							1
2							2

(b) How would Accounts Receivable be shown on the balance sheet on December 31, 1990?

_____

_____

_____

4. *(Cont'd.)*

(c) On December 31, 1990, the account of Barbara Elliott, a customer of the Coda Chemical Company, appeared as follows:

NAME **Barbara Elliott**

ADDRESS **12183 South Union Drive**

DATE		ITEM	POST. REF.	DEBIT	CREDIT	BALANCE
1990 June	5		S14	1 6 0 0 00		1 6 0 0 00

On January 7, 1991, write off Elliott's account, which is determined to be uncollectible. Post to the accounts receivable ledger.

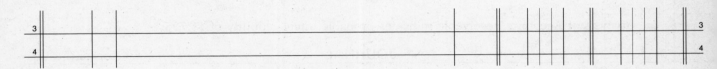

(d) On April 5, 1991, reinstate the account of Elliott written off on January 7. Received $1,600 in full settlement of account. Post to the accounts receivable ledger.

5. *Estimating amount uncollectible.*

The balances in the following accounts for Wang Publishing Company are those for June 30, the end of the fiscal year prior to adjustments. Prepare the necessary adjusting entry for uncollectible accounts in each of the following cases. (Consider each case independently.)

ACCOUNT **Accounts Receivable**   ACCOUNT NO. **131**

DATE		ITEM	POST. REF.	DEBIT	CREDIT	BALANCE DEBIT	BALANCE CREDIT
19-- June	30	Balance				15 2 0 0 00	

5. *(Cont'd.)*

ACCOUNT **Allowance for Doubtful Accounts**   ACCOUNT NO. **131.1**

DATE		ITEM	POST. REF.	DEBIT	CREDIT	BALANCE	
						DEBIT	CREDIT
19-- June	30	Balance				1 4 0 00	

ACCOUNT **Sales**   ACCOUNT NO. **511**

DATE		ITEM	POST. REF.	DEBIT	CREDIT	BALANCE	
						DEBIT	CREDIT
19-- June	30	Balance					153 0 0 0 00

ACCOUNT **Sales Returns and Allowances**   ACCOUNT NO. **512**

DATE		ITEM	POST. REF.	DEBIT	CREDIT	BALANCE	
						DEBIT	CREDIT
19-- June	30	Balance				3 8 0 0 00	

(a) Analysis of Accounts Receivable indicates probable uncollectibility of $1,735.

JOURNAL   PAGE

	DATE	DESCRIPTION	POST. REF.	DEBIT	CREDIT	
1						1
2						2

(b) Losses are estimated at 2% of net sales.

3						3
4						4

(c) Assume the same facts as in (a) except that Allowance for Doubtful Accounts has a credit balance of $95.

5						5
6						6

(d) Assume the same facts as in (b) and a $95 credit in Allowance for Doubtful Accounts.

7						7
8						8

6. *Direct write-off.*

The following accounts receivable account of the CLC Company shows $305 owed by Marsha Chamblee since May 5, 19--. It has been decided that this amount will never be collected.

ACCOUNT **Accounts Receivable**   ACCOUNT NO. **112**

DATE		ITEM	POST. REF.	DEBIT	CREDIT	BALANCE	
						DEBIT	CREDIT
19-- Nov.	30	Balance	✔			17 4 0 0 00	

ACCOUNT **Uncollectible Accounts Expense**   ACCOUNT NO. **612**

DATE		ITEM	POST. REF.	DEBIT	CREDIT	BALANCE	
						DEBIT	CREDIT

NAME   **Marsha Chamblee**

ADDRESS   **907 Broadway Street**

DATE		ITEM	POST. REF.	DEBIT	CREDIT	BALANCE
19-- May	5		S17	3 0 5 00		3 0 5 00

(a) Prepare a journal entry writing off Chamblee's balance on November 30 when it is decided that the amount is uncollectible. Post this entry to the accounts above.

JOURNAL   PAGE **11**

	DATE		DESCRIPTION	POST. REF.	DEBIT	CREDIT	
1							1
2							2
3							3
4							4

Chapter 8 (Continued)

6. *(Cont'd.)*

(b) Assuming Chamblee pays her account in full on December 21 of the same fiscal year, prepare the entries to reinstate the account and record the receipt of payment.

(c) If Chamblee pays her account in full on January 11 of the following year, prepare the entries to reinstate the account and record the receipt of payment.

7. *Temporary investments.*

The Juarez Company has a portfolio of the following short-term marketable equity securities (all common stocks) on December 31, 19--.

Stock	No. of Shares and Cost	Aggregate Cost	Market
R Co.	4,000 @ $12	$ 48,000	$ 53,000
T Co.	2,000 @ 8	16,000	13,000
V Co.	2,600 @ 30	78,000	74,300
		$142,000	$140,300

(a) Prepare the adjusting entry required on December 31, 19--, to reduce the securities from cost to market.

JOURNAL

PAGE

	DATE	DESCRIPTION	POST. REF.	DEBIT	CREDIT	
1						1
2						2
3						3
4						4
5						5

(b) How should the information appear on Juarez's balance sheet and income statement?

Chapter 9

INVENTORIES

Notes from lecture and study:

1. *Effect of errors in accounting for merchandise.*

Indicate the effect of the following errors on the ending inventory, cost of merchandise sold, net income, and owner's equity by writing "over," "under," or "none" in the appropriate column.

Error	Ending Inventory	Cost of Merchandise Sold	Net Income	Owner's Equity
(a) The beginning inventory is understated.				
(b) The ending inventory is overstated.				
(c) Purchases Returns and Allowances were overstated.				
(d) Ending inventory is understated.				
(e) There is an understatement of purchases.				
(f) In taking a physical count at the end of the year, one rack of merchandise was counted twice.				
(g) There is an overstatement of beginning inventory.				
(h) It was discovered that six cases of inventory on one of the docks were not counted (included) in the ending inventory.				

2. *Determining periodic inventory cost (fifo, lifo, and average cost).*

Zapers

					Sold during February	1,200 units
Feb.	1 Balance	1,000 @	$4.00	$4,000		
	6	300 @	4.25	1,275		
	22	600 @	4.50	2,700		
	27	500 @	4.60	2,300		

(a) The subsidiary ledger account for Zapers is given above for the month of February. Determine the cost of the ending inventory by the following methods. (Periodic inventories are kept.)

(1) First-in, first-out

_____

_____

_____

_____

(2) Last-in, first-out.

_____

_____

_____

_____

_____

2. *(Cont'd.)*

(a) (3) Average cost.

_____

_____

_____

_____

(b) Determine the cost of merchandise sold for February if the fifo method is used.

_____

_____

_____

_____

(c) Determine the cost of merchandise sold for February if the lifo method is used.

_____

_____

_____

_____

(d) Assuming a perpetual inventory is kept and that all the sales for the month were made on February 16 at $9 per unit, prepare the entries, in general journal form, to record the sales and cost of goods sold on a fifo basis.

JOURNAL   PAGE

	DATE		DESCRIPTION	POST. REF.	DEBIT	CREDIT	
1							1
2							2
3							3
4							4
5							5
6							6
7							7
8							8
9							9
10							10
11							11
12							12
13							13

3. *Valuation at lower of cost or market.*

(a) The Tillery T-Shirt Shop has the items below in its inventory on November 30. Complete the schedule, and determine the value of the company's inventory using the lower of cost or market.

Item	Inventory Count	Unit Cost	Unit Market	Total Cost	Total Market
B	330	$1.35	$1.40	_____	_____
R	400	2.80	2.65	_____	_____
A	280	3.20	3.30	_____	_____
D	190	1.60	1.50	_____	_____
				_____	_____

(b) Assume the valuation procedure is applied to individual items.

_____

_____

_____

_____

_____

_____

_____

_____

_____

(c) Assume the valuation procedure is applied to the inventory as a whole.

_____

_____

_____

_____

_____

_____

_____

4. *Perpetual inventory record and entries.*

Data purchases and sales of commodity RQ13 are given for the month of July. Inventory of RQ13 on July 1 was 120 units at $6.

July	3	Purchase	140 units @ $ 6.20
	7	Sale	150 units @ 12.00
	10	Purchase	100 units @ 6.30
	12	Sale	110 units @ 12.00
	18	Sale	60 units @ 12.00
	24	Purchase	80 units @ 6.40
	29	Sale	75 units @ 12.00

4. *(Cont'd.)*

(a) Record the purchases and sales of RQ13 for the month of July on the perpetual inventory record given below using the first-in, first-out method.

COMMODITY RQ13									
	PURCHASES			COST OF MERCHANDISE SOLD			INVENTORY		
DATE	QUANTITY	UNIT COST	TOTAL COST	QUANTITY	UNIT COST	TOTAL COST	QUANTITY	UNIT COST	TOTAL COST
July 1							120	6.00	720

(b) Prepare the entries, in general journal form, to record the following transactions:

July 10. Purchased 100 units on account.

JOURNAL   PAGE

	DATE	DESCRIPTION	POST. REF.	DEBIT	CREDIT	
1						1
2						2
3						3

July 12. Sold 110 units on account.

4						4
5						5
6						6
7						7
8						8
9						9
10						10

4. (b) *(Cont'd.)*

July 18. Sold 60 units on account.

11								11
12								12
13								13
14								14
15								15
16								16
17								17
18								18
19								19

(c) Record the purchases and sales of RQ13 for the month of July in the following perpetual inventory record using the last-in, first-out method.

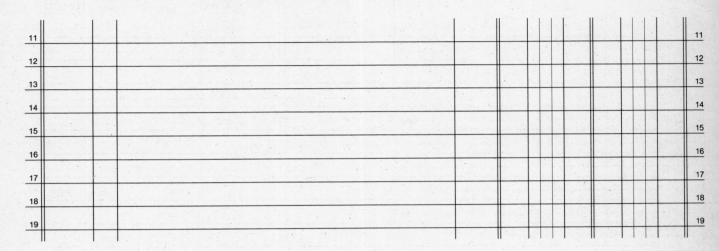

COMMODITY   RQ13

DATE	PURCHASES			COST OF MERCHANDISE SOLD			INVENTORY		
	QUANTITY	UNIT COST	TOTAL COST	QUANTITY	UNIT COST	TOTAL COST	QUANTITY	UNIT COST	TOTAL COST
July 1							120	6.00	720

5. *Retail method of inventory costing.*

The following account balances were taken from the ledger of Gullia's Magic Shop on December 31, 1990.

Merchandise Inventory, January 1, 1990—cost	$153,600
Merchandise Inventory, January 1, 1990—retail	256,000
Purchases—cost	444,000
Purchases—retail	740,000
Sales	592,800
Sales Returns and Allowances	12,800

5. *(Cont'd.)*

Determine the inventory on December 31, 1990, for Gullia's Magic Shop using the retail method.

	Cost	Retail

6. *Gross profit method of estimating inventories.*

G. J.'s Candy Shop was seriously damaged by fire on September 11. The safe was fireproof, and the following information was obtained from the records. Merchandise inventory on January 1 was $37,400. Purchases since January 1 were $84,400, and purchases returns and allowances were $3,400. Sales for the year total $139,600; sales returns and allowances were $5,600. The company's average gross profit rate over the past three years is 45%. Merchandise costing $8,600 was not damaged by the fire; all other merchandise was destroyed.

Using the gross profit method, determine the cost of the merchandise destroyed.

Notes from lecture and study:

Chapter 10 (Continued)

1. *Allocating expenditures to plant asset accounts.*

Assign each expenditure listed below to Land, Land Improvements, Buildings, Equipment, or Other Accounts by placing a check mark (✔) in the appropriate column.

Expenditure	Land	Land Improvements	Buildings	Equipment	Other Accounts
(a) Land acquired for building site.					
(b) Broker's fee and title on land acquired.					
(c) Cost of landscaping for new plant.					
(d) Delinquent property taxes on land acquired.					
(e) Current year property taxes on land.					
(f) Installing security lights around parking lot.					
(g) Architect fees on building constructed.					
(h) Insurance during construction of building.					
(i) Cost of new tires for three-year-old company van.					
(j) Cost incurred on truck caused by wreck.					
(k) Invoice on equipment purchased.					
(l) Transportation charges on equipment.					
(m) Cost of clearing and grading land.					
(n) Cost of installing new equipment.					
(o) Sales taxes on equipment purchased.					

2. *Computing and recording depreciation.*

(a) Using the straight-line method, compute the annual depreciation on an airplane purchased on January 2 for $246,000. The airplane has an expected life of 8 years and an estimated salvage value of $6,000.

(b) Prepare the journal entry to record depreciation on December 31, the end of the first year.

JOURNAL

PAGE

	DATE		DESCRIPTION	POST. REF.	DEBIT	CREDIT	
1							1
2							2
3							3

(c) How would the airplane and accumulated depreciation be shown on the balance sheet at the end of the first year?

_____

_____

_____

_____

_____

_____

_____

at the end of the third year?

_____

_____

_____

_____

_____

_____

_____

Chapter 10 (Continued)

3. *Depreciation methods.*

The Kueter Printing Company purchased a printer at a cost of $144,000 on January 1, the beginning of the fiscal year. The printer has an estimated life of 5 years and an estimated salvage value of $24,000. The printer is expected to produce 20,000,000 copies during its life.

Determine the annual depreciation for each of the first two years and the accumulated depreciation and book value of the printer at the end of each year by the following methods:

(a) Straight-line method.

Year	Depreciation Expense	Accumulated Depreciation	Book Value
1			
2			

(b) Units-of-production method.

Year	Copies Printed	Depreciation Expense	Accumulated Depreciation	Book Value
1	3,500,000			
2	4,000,000			

(c) Declining-balance method (at twice the straight-line rate).

Year	Depreciation Expense	Accumulated Depreciation	Book Value
1			
2			

(d) Sum-of-the-years-digits method.

Year	Depreciation Expense	Accumulated Depreciation	Book Value
1			
2			

(e) MACRS. (Use appropriate table in text.)

Year	Depreciation Expense	Accumulated Depreciation	Book Value
1			
2			

3. *(Cont'd.)*

(f) Assuming the printer was purchased on July 1, determine the depreciation expense, accumulated depreciation, and book value at the end of each of the first two years by the sum-of-the-years-digits.

Year	Depreciation Expense	Accumulated Depreciation	Book Value
1	_____	_____	_____
2	_____	_____	_____

4. *Revision of depreciation.*

Ingram Orchards purchased a truck on January 2, 1987, at a cost of $38,000. The truck had an estimated useful life of 8 years and an estimated residual value of $6,000. Depreciation was recorded for the first three years by the straight-line method. On January 2, 1990, Ingram Orchards determined the estimated useful life of the truck to be a total of 12 years (from January 2, 1987) with an estimated residual value of $3,000.

(a) Prepare the journal entry to record the depreciation expense on December 31, 1990, based on the revised estimates.

JOURNAL

PAGE

	DATE	DESCRIPTION	POST. REF.	DEBIT	CREDIT	
1						1
2						2
3						3
4						4
5						5

Chapter 10 (Continued)

4. *(Cont'd.)*

   (b) Show how the truck and accumulated depreciation would be shown on the balance sheet on December 31, 1990.

_____

_____

_____

_____

_____

_____

_____

_____

_____

_____

5. *Disposal and exchange of plant assets.*

   (a) Journalize the discarding of equipment after its fifteenth year of life if it cost $300,000, has a life of 15 years, and has no scrap value.

JOURNAL

PAGE

	DATE	DESCRIPTION	POST. REF.	DEBIT	CREDIT	
1						1
2						2

   (b) Journalize the discarding of the equipment in (a) at the end of the eleventh year assuming straight-line depreciation.

   (c) Record the sale of the equipment in (a) at the end of the tenth year for $115,000 cash.

5. *(Cont'd.)*

(d) Record the sale of the equipment in (a) at the end of 7½ years for $142,000 cash.

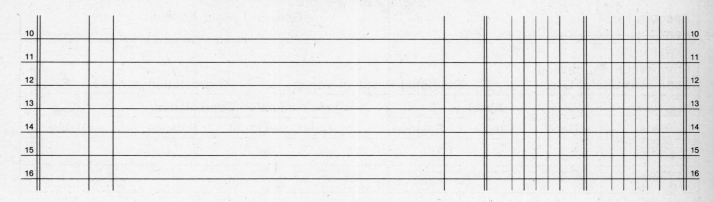

(e) Prepare the entry if the equipment in (a) is traded in at the end of 10 years on new equipment with a cost of $340,000. A trade-in allowance of $120,000 is granted with the difference paid in cash.

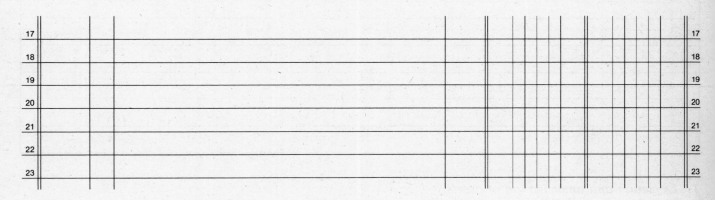

(f) Prepare the journal entry in (e) if the trade-in allowance is $90,000.

6. *Subsidiary ledger for plant assets.*

Benjy Butchers purchased a meat counter (store equipment) from Marshall Company on January 2, 1990, at a cost of $13,000. The counter had an estimated useful life of 12 years and a $1,000 trade-in value.

Fill in the plant asset record for the meat counter through December 31, 1993. The account number is 23-7. Benjy uses the straight-line method of depreciation.

6. *(Cont'd.)*

<table>
<tr><td colspan="8" align="center">Plant Asset Record</td><td></td></tr>
<tr><td colspan="4">Account No.:
Item:</td><td colspan="5">General Ledger Account:</td></tr>
<tr><td colspan="2">Serial No.:
From Whom Purchased:
Estimated Useful Life:</td><td colspan="2">Estimated Residual Value:</td><td colspan="5">Depreciation per Year:</td></tr>
</table>

| Date | Asset | | | Accumulated Depreciation | | | Book Value |
	Debit	Credit	Balance	Debit	Credit	Balance	

7. *Depletion and amortization of assets.*

(a) The Jesse Mining Company purchased a copper mine in 1990 for $48,000,000. The mine has an estimated 1,500,000 tons of coal. After mining, the property is expected to have a residual value of $3,000,000. Prepare the entry to record the depletion for the first year if 600,000 tons of coal are mined and sold.

JOURNAL   PAGE

	DATE	DESCRIPTION	POST. REF.	DEBIT	CREDIT	
1						1
2						2

(b) Washington Kitchen Equipment purchased a patent for a new high-speed mixer at a cost of $42,000. It is estimated that the patent will be useful for only 6 years. Prepare the entry to record the amortization of the patent at the end of the first full year.

Notes from lecture and study:

Chapter 11 (Continued)

1. *Payroll computations.*

Nazar Talib, a maintenance foreman for Swifton Products, is employed at an hourly rate of $10.40, receiving time and one-half for all hours over 40 each week. The following payroll data are available:

Hours worked this week	44 hours
Earnings this year up to current payroll period	$6,720.00
Federal income tax withheld this week	$ 95.68
FICA tax rate	7.5%
Unemployment tax rates:	
Federal	0.8%
State	5.4%

(a) What are Talib's gross earnings this week? _____

(b) How much FICA tax will be withheld from his pay? _____

(c) What is the amount of Talib's net earnings? _____

(d) Prepare the general journal entry to record Talib's payroll on the books of his employer.

JOURNAL   PAGE

	DATE	DESCRIPTION	POST. REF.	DEBIT	CREDIT	
1						1
2						2
3						3
4						4
5						5

(e) What is the amount of unemployment tax to be paid by the employer for

State _____

Federal _____

(f) Prepare the journal entry to record the employer's payroll tax expense for the period.

6						6
7						7
8						8
9						9
10						10

2. *Determination of profit-sharing bonus.*

Sara Sloan is a vice-president for the Camden Container Company and, in addition to her annual salary, is paid an 8% profit-sharing bonus at the end of the year.

Determine Sloan's bonus at the end of the current year under each assumption on the following page if Camden Container reported an income of $960,000 before deducting bonus or income taxes. Income taxes are levied at a rate of 40% of income.

124

2. *(Cont'd.)*

(a) Bonus is based on income before deducting bonus and taxes.

(b) Bonus is based on income after deducting bonus but before taxes.

(c) Bonus is based on income before deducting bonus but after deducting taxes.

(d) Bonus is based on net income after deducting bonus and taxes.

3. *Preparing the payroll.*

(a) Complete the payroll form below for Los Cuartos for the week ended December 9. Johnston and Cross authorized a U.S. bond deduction of $10 per week, and everyone authorized a $5 deduction for the United Fund Drive except Bott, who authorized $8. The overtime rate is 1 1/2 times the regular rate for all hours over 40 a week. Evans and Johnston's salaries are charged to Office Salaries Expense and all other salaries to Sales Salaries Expense. Unemployment compensation tax is at the rate of .8% for federal and 5.4% for state on the first $7,000 of salary for the year. Deduct FICA tax at the rate of 7.5% on the first $50,000. Begin with Check No. 741.

PAYROLL FOR WEEK ENDING DEC. 9, 19--

LEFT PAGE

NAME	Hourly Rate	Cumulative Earnings	Total Hours	EARNINGS Regular	EARNINGS Overtime	EARNINGS Total	TAXABLE EARNINGS Unemployment Comp.	TAXABLE EARNINGS FICA
1 T. Evans	6.50	$ 5,190	42					
2 D. Johnston	9.20	6,770	44					
3 C. Lamberth	10.00	6,920	40					
4 P. Cross	13.00	26,440	46					
5 S. Bott	20.00	49,000	51					
TOTALS								

RIGHT PAGE

	DEDUCTIONS FICA Tax	DEDUCTIONS Federal Income Tax	DEDUCTIONS Group Insurance	DEDUCTIONS U.S. Bonds	DEDUCTIONS United Fund	DEDUCTIONS Total	PAID Net Amount	PAID Check No.	ACCOUNTS DEBITED Sales Salaries Expense	ACCOUNTS DEBITED Office Salaries Expense
1		55.20	8.00							
2		73.60	8.00							
3		80.00	8.00							
4		127.40	8.00							
5		208.00	8.00							
TOTALS										

3. *(Cont'd.)*

(b) Prepare the entry to record the payroll for Los Curatos in the general journal.

JOURNAL

PAGE

	DATE		DESCRIPTION	POST. REF.	DEBIT	CREDIT	
1							1
2							2
3							3
4							4
5							5
6							6
7							7
8							8

(c) Record the payment of the payroll in (a) assuming Check No. 867 is written on December 10 to transfer sufficient funds to a special payroll bank account and that payroll checks 741-745 are written to the employees.

CASH PAYMENTS JOURNAL

PAGE

	DATE	CK. NO.	ACCOUNT DEBITED	POST. REF.	SUNDRY ACCOUNTS DR.	ACCOUNTS PAYABLE DR.	PURCHASES DISCOUNT CR.	CASH CR.	
1									1
2									2
3									3
4									4
5									5

(d) Record, in general journal form, the entry to record Los Curatos' payroll tax expense for the week.

9							9
10							10
11							11
12							12
13							13
14							14
15							15
16							16

Chapter 11 (Continued)

4. *Recording the payroll.*

Selected totals from the payroll record of Stelchek Service Company for the month of April are given below.

Sales salaries	$32,800	Taxable earnings:	
Office salaries	9,400	Unemployment compensation	$14,800
Total salaries	$42,200	FICA	42,200

Deductions:		Tax rates:	
Income tax	$7,385	FICA	7.5%
Group insurance	420	State unemployment	5.4%
Accounts receivable	530	Federal unemployment	.8%

Prepare the following entries, in general journal form, for Stelcheck Service Company.

(a) To record the payroll for the month of April.

JOURNAL

PAGE

	DATE	DESCRIPTION	POST. REF.	DEBIT	CREDIT	
1						1
2						2
3						3
4						4
5						5
6						6
7						7
8						8
9						9
10						10

(b) To record the employer's payroll tax expense on the April payroll.

11						11
12						12
13						13
14						14
15						15
16						16
17						17
18						18
19						19
20						20

5. *Notes payable and interest expense.*

Jean Sheehan gave a 120-day, 10% note payable to Delta Motors in payment of her account of $9,000 on October 2, 1990. On December 31, 1990, the following ledger accounts were provided before adjustments. Sheehan had no other notes payable at this time.

ACCOUNT **Interest Payable**   ACCOUNT NO. **22**

DATE	ITEM	POST. REF.	DEBIT	CREDIT	BALANCE DEBIT	BALANCE CREDIT

ACCOUNT **Interest Expense**   ACCOUNT NO. **72**

DATE	ITEM	POST. REF.	DEBIT	CREDIT	BALANCE DEBIT	BALANCE CREDIT

(a) Prepare the adjusting entry necessary on Sheehan's books on December 31, 1990, and post.

JOURNAL   PAGE **31**

DATE	DESCRIPTION	POST. REF.	DEBIT	CREDIT
1				
2				

(b) Prepare the entry necessary to close Interest Expense on December 31, 1990, and post.

3				
4				

(c) Prepare the reversing entry necessary on January 1, 1991, and post.

5				
6				

(d) Prepare the entry on January 30, 1991, when Sheehan pays the note plus interest and post.

7				
8				
9				

5. *(Cont'd.)*

(e) Prepare the entry required on January 30, 1991, when payment is made if the reversing entry has not been made.

6. *Issuing and discounting notes payable.*

Prepare the necessary entries, in general journal form, for the following transactions related to notes payable for Jarrod Kersey.

April 12. Issued a $5,000, 60-day, 9% note to the Imke Company in payment of his account.

JOURNAL

PAGE

	DATE	DESCRIPTION	POST. REF.	DEBIT	CREDIT	
1						1
2						2

June 11. Paid the note due to Imke plus interest.

September 23. Kersey discounted his own $7,400, 90-day, non-interest-bearing note (dated today) at Castle Bank at 12%.

December 22. Kersey paid the maturity value of the note discounted at the bank.

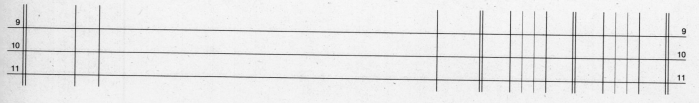

7. *Other current liabilities.*

Prepare the following adjusting entries relating to current liabilities for the Cleveland Company on December 31.

(a) Record the estimated total amount of the current month's vacation pay, $1,140.

JOURNAL   PAGE **12**

	DATE		DESCRIPTION	POST. REF.	DEBIT	CREDIT	
1							1
2							2
3							3
4							4
5							5
6							6
7							7

(b) Cleveland maintains a pension plan for its employees. The pension plan has a pension cost for the current year of $24,600. Cleveland pays $18,500 to the fund trustee, Capital Trust Company. Prepare the entry to record the pension cost and payment for the current year.

8							8
9							9
10							10
11							11
12							12
13							13

(c) Cleveland warrants its products for one year; the product warranty is 4% of sales. Record the accrued product warranty at the end of December if the sales for the month were $510,000.

14							14
15							15
16							16
17							17
18							18
19							19
20							20
21							21

Chapter 12   CONCEPTS AND PRINCIPLES

Notes from lecture and study:

1. *Accounting concepts and principles.*

In the left column, a list of basic accounting concepts and principles is presented. In the right column are statements or situations regarding accounting data. Determine which concept or principle is most involved or appropriate to the statement or situation, and write the identifying letter in the space provided. (Note: Concepts and principles may be used for more than one answer.)

Concepts & Principles	Statement or Situation	Answer
	1. Use of footnotes in the financial statements.	1. _____
A. Accounting Period	2. Supports the treatment of prepaid expenses as assets.	2. _____
B. Adequate Disclosure	3. Anticipates no profits and provides for all losses.	3. _____
C. Business Entity		
D. Conservatism	4. Allows comparison of financial data from period to period.	4. _____
E. Consistency		
F. Cost	5. Interested persons should be able to assume that successive financial statements are based on the same generally accepted accounting principles.	5. _____
G. Going Concern		
H. Matching Revenue and Expired Costs	6. Accounting records and data reported on financial statements should be based on information that is completely objective and subject to verification.	6. _____
I. Materiality		
J. Objective Evidence	7. The amount of cash or equivalent given to acquire the property or service.	7. _____
K. Recognition of Revenue		
L. Unit of Measure	8. Use of the installment sales method.	8. _____
	9. Assets = Liabilities + Owner's Equity.	9. _____
	10. Relative importance of any event or accounting procedure that affects items on the financial statements.	10. _____
	11. The maximum interval between financial reports is one year.	11. _____
	12. The necessity for adjusting entries at the end of the period.	12. _____
	13. Determining the expired costs to be allocated to the period.	13. _____
	14. In selecting among alternatives, accountants often favor the method or procedure that yields the lesser amount of net income or of asset value.	14. _____
	15. The use of checks, invoices, and contracts to make entries in the accounting records.	15. _____
	16. Recording revenue at the point of sale.	16. _____
	17. All business transactions are recorded in terms of money.	17. _____
	18. Assumption that a business entity has a reasonable expectation of continuing in business for an indefinite period of time.	18. _____
	19. Assumption that a business enterprise is separate and distinct from the persons who supply its assets.	19. _____
	20. Financial statements should contain all of the pertinent data believed essential to the reader's understanding of the enterprise's financial status.	20. _____

Chapter 12 (Continued)

2. *Installment method of recognizing revenue.*

(a) From the following information, determine the gross profit percentages for the period 1990-1992 for the Apache Company.

	Installment Sales	Cost of Merchandise Sold	Gross Profit	Gross Profit %
1990	$1,400,000	$ 770,000	_____	_____
1991	$1,600,000	$ 960,000	_____	_____
1992	$2,200,000	$1,430,000	_____	_____

(b) The beginning and ending balances of installment accounts receivable for 1992 are listed below. Determine the amount collected.

1-1-92	12-31-92	Amount Collected
from 1990 sales—$280,000	from 1990 sales—$ —0—	_____
from 1991 sales—$500,000	from 1992 sales—$ 200,000	_____
	from 1992 sales—$ 900,000	_____
$780,000	$1,100,000	

(c) Determine the amount of gross profit that would be realized in 1992 if Apache uses the installment method of recognizing revenue.

(d) Determine the amount of gross profit that would be realized in 1992 if Apache uses the point-of-sale method of recognizing revenue.

3. *Recognition of revenue.*

For each of the following items, show the dollar amount of revenue that should be reported in 1991 and 1992. Record your answers in the spaces provided.

	1991	1992
(a)		
(b)		
(c)		
(d)		
(e)		

(a) On September 1, 1991, a training facility was subleased. One year's rent of $18,000 was received in advance.

(b) Subscriptions to *Advance Magazine* received beginning November 1, 1991, for a six-month period in the amount of $24,000. Payment is due April 1992.

(c) Season tickets in the amount of $272,000 for a series of eight concerts were sold on December 1, 1991, the beginning of the season. Two concerts are held each month through March 1992.

(d) The contract is set on March 27, 1989, for building a veterinary clinic at a price of $3,600,000. During 1991 the clinic is estimated to be 40% completed, and the costs incurred total $1,000,000. The clinic is completed in 1992 at a total cost of $2,500,000.

(e) On October 2, 1990, $60,000 was loaned at 10% for 120 days.

4. *Percentage-of-contract-completion method of recognizing revenue.*

The Kistler Construction Company was awarded a contract to construct a new drive-in facility for Lewisville National Bank at a contract price of $6,300,000. Construction began in 1989 and was completed in 1991. The transactions relating to the contract are summarized below.

	1989	1990	1991
Costs incurred during the year	$ 562,500	$1,687,500	$1,125,000
Estimated costs for completion	2,812,500	1,125,000	—0—
Payments received during the year...	675,000	2,475,000	2,250,000

Determine the amount of revenue and the income to be recognized each year. Revenue is to be recognized by the percentage-of-contract-completion method.

_____

_____

_____

_____

_____

_____

_____

_____

_____

_____

_____

_____

_____

_____

Chapter 12 (Continued)

5. *Accounting for price-level changes.*

Ahmed Kridli purchased 82 acres of land for $102,000 at a time when the price-level was 100. On September 11 of the current year when the price-level index was 120, the land was sold for $175,000.

(a) How much of the gain would be realized by Ahmed according to conventional accounting?

(b) How much of the gain is attributable to the change in purchasing power?

(c) How much of the gain is considered a true gain in terms of current dollars?

Notes from lecture and study.

Chapter 13 (Continued)

1. *Recording partners' investments.*

Gladys and Richard form a partnership on September 1. Gladys agrees to transfer the following assets and liabilities to the partnership as her investment: cash, $7,520; accounts receivable, $13,200; equipment, $84,000 (cost); accumulated depreciation, $23,600; accounts payable, $8,100; and notes payable, $8,000. The partners agree that allowance for doubtful accounts should be 10% of accounts receivable and that the equipment is worth only 40% of its original cost.

Richard is to invest $55,000 in cash.

Prepare the necessary entries, in general journal form, to record the investments of Gladys and Richard on the books of the partnership.

JOURNAL   PAGE

	DATE	DESCRIPTION	POST. REF.	DEBIT	CREDIT	
1						1
2						2
3						3
4						4
5						5
6						6
7						7
8						8
9						9
10						10
11						11
12						12

2. *Division of net income or net loss.*

Mary Ann and Walter form a partnership with investments of $200,000 and $300,000 respectively. Determine their participation in net income of $80,000 under each of the following assumptions:

	Mary Ann	**Walter**
(a) No agreement.		
	_____	_____
(b) Ratio of beginning capital balances.		
	_____	_____

2. *(Cont'd.)*

	Mary Ann	**Walter**

(c) Interest on original capital of 12%, the remainder equally.

_____ _____

(d) Salaries of $20,000 for Mary Ann and $15,000 for Walter, the remainder in a ratio of the beginning capital balances.

_____ _____

(e) Interest of 12% on the original capital, salaries of $10,000 and $5,000 respectively, and the remainder equally.

_____ _____

(f) Same agreement as (e) assuming a net income of $40,000.

_____ _____

(g) Same agreement as (e) assuming a net loss of $20,000.

_____ _____

3. *Income division, closing entries, and statement of owner's equity.*

A portion of the ledger for the Sanderson Garden Shop after all expense and revenue accounts have been closed is given below.

Janae, Capital		Krista, Capital		Philip, Capital	
	1/1 100,000		1/1 80,000		1/1 120,000

Janae, Drawing		Krista, Drawing		Philip, Drawing	
10,000		13,000		7,500	

Income Summary	
	103,000

The profit-sharing agreement provides for interest of 10% on beginning capital balances, salaries of $10,000 for Krista and $15,000 for Philip, and the remainder in a 3:2:1 ratio to Janae, Krista, and Philip respectively.

(a) Prepare a schedule showing the distribution of income to the partners.

_____

_____

_____

_____

_____

_____

_____

_____

_____

(b) Prepare the general journal entry to close the income summary account.

JOURNAL

PAGE

	DATE	DESCRIPTION	POST. REF.	DEBIT	CREDIT	
1						1
2						2
3						3
4						4
5						5
6						6
7						7
8						8

3. *(Cont'd.)*

(c) Prepare the general journal entry to close the drawing accounts.

9							9
10							10
11							11
12							12
13							13
14							14

(d) Prepare a statement of owner's equity for the year.

4. *Admission of a partner.*

Don and Pam are partners in The Wee-One Day Care Center with capital balances of $45,000 and $30,000 respectively. They share profits equally. Record the admission of Juanita to the partnership under the following conditions:

(a) Juanita purchased one-third of Don and Pam's interest by personally paying them $15,000 and $10,000.

JOURNAL

PAGE

	DATE	DESCRIPTION	POST. REF.	DEBIT	CREDIT	
1						1
2						2
3						3
4						4
5						5

Chapter 13 (Continued)

4. *(Cont'd.)*

(b) Juanita invests $25,000 for a one-fourth interest in the partnership.

(c) Juanita invests $25,000 for a 20% interest recognizing goodwill of $25,000 attributable to the old partners.

(d) Juanita invests $25,000 for a one-third interest recognizing goodwill of $12,500 attributable to the new partner.

5. *Liquidating a partnership.*

Anne, Walt, and Heff are partners with a profit-sharing agreement of 3:2:1. After closing the accounts in anticipation of liquidating the partnership, the following trial balance was taken:

Cash	3,400	
Accounts Receivable (net)	56,400	
Merchandise Inventory	51,700	
Equipment	152,600	
Accumulated Depreciation		52,600
Accounts Payable		72,300
Anne, Capital		60,800
Walt, Capital		32,400
Heff, Capital		46,000
	264,100	264,100

Additional Data: Accounts receivable are sold to the bank for $32,400. The merchandise inventory realized $23,200 in an auction, and the equipment sold for $46,000. The accounts payable are paid in full. If any partner is deficient, it is assumed that that partner will not be able to make it up. Therefore, the deficiency must be absorbed by the remaining partners.

5. *(Cont'd.)*

(a) Prepare a statement schedule of partnership liquidation using the form provided below.

(b) Prepare the necessary journal entries on the following page.

	Cash +	Noncash Assets +	Liabilities =	Capital		
				Anne 50% (3/6) +	Walt 33⅓% (2/6) +	Heff 16⅔% (1/6)
Balances before realization	$3,400	$208,100	$72,300	$60,800	$32,400	$46,000

5. *(Cont'd.)*

JOURNAL

	DATE		DESCRIPTION	POST. REF.	DEBIT	CREDIT	
1							1
2							2
3							3
4							4
5							5
6							6
7							7
8							8
9							9
10							10
11							11
12							12
13							13
14							14
15							15
16							16
17							17
18							18
19							19
20							20
21							21
22							22
23							23
24							24
25							25
26							26
27							27
28							28
29							29
30							30
31							31
32							32

Notes from lecture and study:

1. *Comparing characteristics of partnerships with corporations.*

   Indicate in the space provided which characteristics apply to corporations and which apply to partnerships (Some items may apply to both.)

	Partnerships	Corporations
(a) Accounting entity	_____	_____
(b) Board of directors	_____	_____
(c) Co-ownership of property	_____	_____
(d) Limited liability of owners	_____	_____
(e) Subject to additional taxes	_____	_____
(f) Limited life	_____	_____
(g) Mutual agency	_____	_____
(h) Participation in income by owners	_____	_____
(i) Stockholders	_____	_____
(j) Separate legal entity	_____	_____
(k) Transferable units of ownership	_____	_____

2. *Computing dividends on preferred and common stock.*

   The Carrie Corporation has outstanding 20,000 shares of 9% cumulative preferred stock, $60 par, and 200,000 shares of common stock, $25 par. Both classes of stock were issued at par. In the first three years of operation, the company earned $165,000, $360,000, and $480,000 respectively. Due to the needs of expansion and growth of new business, the board of directors maintained a policy of distributing only one-half of the earnings each year. (When necessary a partial dividend will be made.)

   (a) Show the distribution of the dividends to preferred and common stock for the Carrie Corporation using the following schedule:

Year	Total Dividends	Preferred	Common
1	_____	_____	_____
2	_____	_____	_____
3	_____	_____	_____
Total	_____	_____	_____

   (b) Compute the total dividends per share for the three-year period for

   Preferred _____

   Common _____

   (c) Assuming that both classes of stock were sold at par at the beginning of the three-year period, determine the total dividends received on an investment of $20,000.

   (1) In preferred stock _____

   (2) In common stock _____

3. *Dividends with cumulative and participating preferred stock.*

On December 31, 1991, the Alexander Corporation had the following balances in its stockholders' equity accounts:

Preferred 8% stock, $10 par (100,000 shares authorized, 30,000
shared issued) . . . . $ 300,000
Paid-in capital in excess of par—preferred stock 30,000
Common stock, $5 par (1,000,000 shares authorized, 300,000
shares issued) 1,500,000
Paid-in capital in excess of par—common stock 655,000
Retained earnings 1,110,000

At the annual stockholders' meeting of the Alexander Corporation, the board of directors declared a cash dividend of $180,000.

Determine the amount of dividends to be paid to the preferred stockholders and the common stockholders in each of the following situations:

(a) The preferred stock is noncumulative, nonparticipating.

Preferred stock _____

Common stock _____

(b) The preferred stock is noncumulative, participating. The preferred stock contract provides that if total dividends to be distributed exceed the regular preferred dividend and a $.50 per share dividend on common, the preferred shall share in the excess ratably on a share-for-share basis with common.

Preferred stock _____

Common stock _____

(c) The preferred stock is cumulative, nonparticipating. No dividends were paid in 1989 or 1990.

Preferred stock _____

Common stock _____

Chapter 14 (Continued)

4. *Issuing stock and other corporate transactions.*

Prepare the necessary entries, in general journal form, to record the following selected transactions of the Yang Corporation. The company was organized on August 1.

(a) Issued 20,000 shares of common stock, $5 par, for $11 per share. There are 450,000 shares of common stock authorized.

JOURNAL

PAGE

	DATE		DESCRIPTION	POST. REF.	DEBIT	CREDIT	
1							1
2							2
3							3
4							4

(b) Issued 15,000 shares of 8% cumulative preferred stock, $18 par, for $15 per share. There are 175,000 shares of preferred stock authorized.

5							5
6							6
7							7
8							8

(c) Paid attorney $6,400 for legal fees in organizing the company.

9							9
10							10
11							11

(d) Issued 85,000 shares of common stock for the following assets: land, $90,000; building, $225,000; inventory, $70,000; and equipment, $150,000.

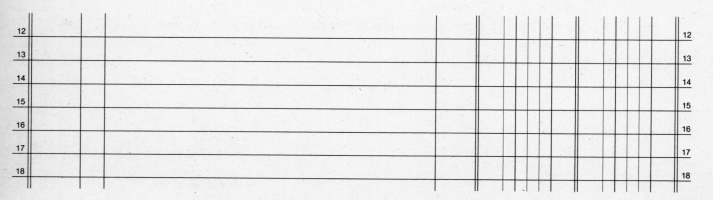

12							12
13							13
14							14
15							15
16							16
17							17
18							18

5. *Stock subscriptions.*

Prepare journal entries for the following transactions.

(a) The Torres Corporation accepted subscriptions to 40,000 shares of $5 par common stock at $14 per share with a down payment of 40%.

JOURNAL   PAGE

	DATE	DESCRIPTION	POST. REF.	DEBIT	CREDIT	
1						1
2						2
3						3
4						4
5						5
6						6
7						7
8						8

(b) Received one-half of the balance from all subscribers.

9						9
10						10
11						11
12						12
13						13
14						14
15						15

(c) Received balance due from all subscribers and issued the stock.

16						16
17						17
18						18
19						19
20						20
21						21
22						22
23						23

Chapter 14 (Continued)

6. *Treasury stock transactions.*

The capital accounts of the Hurley Corporation are as follows:

Common stock, $6 par (300,000 shares authorized) $900,000
Excess of issue price over par 300,000
Retained earnings 530,000

(a) Record the following transactions for the year for the Hurley Corporation involving its own stock.

(1) Purchased 4,000 shares of treasury stock for $10 per share.

JOURNAL

PAGE

	DATE	DESCRIPTION	POST. REF.	DEBIT	CREDIT	
1						1
2						2
3						3

(2) Sold 2,000 shares purchased in (1) for $13 per share.

(3) Sold 500 shares purchased in (1) for $8 per share.

(b) After the above transactions have been completed, compute the number of shares of the Hurley Corporation for each of the following:

Authorized _____

Issued _____

Outstanding _____

7. *Equity per share.*

Compute the equity <u>per share</u> for each class of stock from the stockholders' equity sections given below.

Common stock, $20 par	$5,000,000
Excess of issue price over par	2,750,000
Retained earnings	950,000
Total stockholders' equity	$8,700,000

_____

(b)
Preferred 7% stock, $25 par	$1,300,000
Excess of issue price over par	450,000
Common stock, $60 par	2,850,000
Deficit	(170,000)
Total stockholders' equity	$4,430,000

Preferred _____

Common _____

(c)
Preferred 8% stock, cumulative, $40 par (liquidating value, $50 per share)	$ 800,000
Common stock, $35 par	2,170,000
Retained earnings	690,000
Total stockholders' equity	$3,660,000

Preferred _____

Common _____

(d) Same as (c) above except dividends on preferred stock are in arrears for two years (plus the current year).

Preferred _____

Common _____

(e) Paid in capital:

Common stock, $20 par (180,000 shares issued)....	$3,600,000
Excess of issue price over par	500,000
Total paid-in capital	$4,100,000
Retained earnings	750,000
Total..	$4,850,000
Less treasury stock (10,000 shares at cost)	200,000
Total stockholders' equity	$4,650,000

Common _____

Chapter 15   STOCKHOLDERS' EQUITY, EARNINGS, AND DIVIDENDS

Notes from lecture and study:

1. *Income tax allocation.*

The Waco Corporation was organized on January 1, 1990. The business was immediately successful, but needs for positive cash flow made it necessary for the company to pay as little as possible in income taxes for the first few years. The difference in accounting methods used caused a variance in income reported for financial statements and income for tax purposes during the first three years of operations as follows:

	1990	1991	1992
Income per books before income tax......	$930,000	$820,000	$780,000
Income per income tax return	620,000	705,000	865,000

Assuming an income tax rate each year of 40%, prepare the entries, in general journal form, necessary to record the income tax liability and the deferred taxes each year for the Waco Corporation.

JOURNAL

PAGE

	DATE		DESCRIPTION	POST. REF.	DEBIT	CREDIT	
1							1
2							2
3							3
4							4
5							5
6							6
7							7
8							8
9							9
10							10
11							11
12							12
13							13
14							14
15							15
16							16
17							17
18							18
19							19
20							20
21							21
22							22
23							23

2. *Income statement and statement of retained earnings.*

You are given a summary of operating data and retained earnings for the Hammer Corporation for the year ended December 31, 1990. The corporation had 100,000 shares of common stock outstanding during the entire year (no preferred).

Retained earnings, unappropriated 1-1-1990	$374,000
Appropriation for plant expansion 1-1-1990	150,000
Sales	920,000
Cost of merchandise sold	417,000
Operating expenses	191,700
Loss from discontinued operations	152,000
Gain on condemnation of property	268,000
Appropriation for plant expansion during 1990	72,000
Cash dividends	145,000
Income tax:	
On income from continuing operations	106,780
On gain on condemnation of property	100,800
Tax savings on loss from discontinued operations	(65,600)

(a) Prepare an income statement for 1990 for the Hammer Corporation including the computations for earnings per share data.

2. *(Cont'd.)*

(b) Prepare a retained earnings statement for the Hammer Corporation for 1990.

Chapter 15 (Continued)

3. *Appropriations of retained earnings.*

The stockholders' equity accounts of Yolanda Foods as of June 1 are as follows:

Common stock, $10 par (35,000 shares issued)	$350,000
Excess of issue price over par	210,000
Appropriation for contingencies	80,000
Retained earnings	405,000
Treasury stock (3,000 shares at cost)	60,000

Prepare the entries, in general journal form, necessary on the following dates:

June 5. Appropriation of retained earnings for treasury stock purchased.

June 14. Reduced the appropriation for contingencies by $25,000.

June 21. Appropriation of retained earnings for plant expansion, $140,000.

June 23. Yolanda sold 1,000 shares of treasury stock for $38,000. Record entry to reduce appropriation of retained earnings for treasury stock.

JOURNAL

PAGE

	DATE	DESCRIPTION	POST. REF.	DEBIT	CREDIT	
1						1
2						2
3						3
4						4
5						5
6						6
7						7
8						8
9						9
10						10
11						11
12						12
13						13
14						14
15						15
16						16
17						17
18						18
19						19
20						20
21						21
22						22

4. *Recording cash and stock dividends.*

The Eagle Express Corporation's balance sheet on November 1, 1990, showed the following balances in stockholders' equity:

Common stock, $8 par	$800,000
Excess of issue price over par	320,000
Retained earnings	650,000

(a) On November 1, 1990, the board of directors declared a cash dividend of $.30 per share to stockholders of record November 15 payable on November 30. Prepare the entries, in general journal form, on each of the following dates:

JOURNAL   PAGE

DATE		DESCRIPTION	POST. REF.	DEBIT	CREDIT
Nov.	1				
	15				
	30				

(b) On February 1, 1991, the Eagle Express Corporation declared a 10% stock dividend payable on February 21. The market price of the stock on February 1 was $12 per share. Prepare the entries, in general journal form, required on the following dates:

JOURNAL   PAGE

DATE		DESCRIPTION	POST. REF.	DEBIT	CREDIT
Feb.	1				
	21				

5. *Cash dividend, stock dividend, and stock split.*

The capital accounts of the Alzado Corporation on March 1 of the current year were as follows:

Common stock, $10 par (1,000,000 shares authorized, 840,000 shares issued)	$8,400,000
Excess of issue price over par	2,720,000
Retained earnings	4,920,000
Appropriation for treasury stock	520,000
Treasury stock (20,000 shares at cost)	(520,000)

Journalize the following selected transactions for the year.

JOURNAL
PAGE

	DATE		DESCRIPTION	POST. REF.	DEBIT	CREDIT	
1	March	4	Declared a 10% stock dividend on the stock out-				1
2			standing at this date. (Market value of the stock is $28.)				2
3			Dividend is payable on April 1.				3
4							4
5							5
6							6
7	April	1	Paid the stock dividend declared above.				7
8							8
9							9
10	April	24	Declared a $.40 per share cash dividend payable on				10
11			May 3.				11
12							12
13							13
14	May	3	Paid the cash dividend.				14
15							15
16							16
17	Nov.	1	The board of directors authorized a stock split of 2 for				17
18			1 with a reduction in par to $5 per share.				18
19							19
20							20
21	Dec.	1	Declared a cash dividend of $.25 per share payable				21
22			December 23.				22
23							23
24							24
25	Dec.	23	Paid the cash dividend.				25
26							26
27							27

6. *Classification of stockholders' equity accounts.*

Indicate by checking the appropriate blank whether each of the following items would be reported on a corporation's balance sheet as (1) paid-in capital, (2) retained earnings, or (3) other.

	Paid-In Capital	Retained Earnings	Other
(a) Appropriation for treasury stock	_____	_____	_____
(b) Cash dividends	_____	_____	_____
(c) Cash dividends payable	_____	_____	_____
(d) Common stock subscribed	_____	_____	_____
(e) Common stock subscriptions receivable	_____	_____	_____
(f) Cumulative effect of change in accounting principle	_____	_____	_____
(g) Deferred income tax payable	_____	_____	_____
(h) Discount on common stock	_____	_____	_____
(i) Excess of issue price of common stock over par	_____	_____	_____
(j) Gain on condemnation of land (extraordinary item)	_____	_____	_____
(k) Gain on redemption of preferred stock	_____	_____	_____
(l) Gain on sale of treasury stock	_____	_____	_____
(m) Income tax payable	_____	_____	_____
(n) Loss on disposal of segment of a business	_____	_____	_____
(o) Net income	_____	_____	_____
(p) Organization cost	_____	_____	_____
(q) Preferred stock (par value)	_____	_____	_____
(r) Premium on preferred stock	_____	_____	_____
(s) Prior period adjustment	_____	_____	_____
(t) Stock dividends distributable	_____	_____	_____
(u) Treasury stock	_____	_____	_____

LONG-TERM LIABILITIES
AND INVESTMENTS IN BONDS

Notes from lecture and study:

_____

_____

_____

_____

_____

_____

_____

_____

_____

_____

_____

_____

_____

_____

_____

_____

_____

_____

_____

_____

_____

_____

_____

_____

_____

1. *Comparing methods of financing.*

The Sioux Corporation is to be organized with total financing of $32,000,000. It is estimated that the total earnings before taxes, interest, or dividends will be $4,000,000 per year. Compare the effects of the following methods of financing on the earnings per share of common stock assuming an average income tax rate of 40%.

	Plan A	Plan B	Plan C
10% bonds	—	—	$10,000,000
Preferred 8% stock	—	$12,000,000	10,000,000
Common stock, $20 par	$32,000,000	20,000,000	12,000,000
Total	$32,000,000	$32,000,000	$32,000,000

Chapter 16 (Continued)

2. *Computation of bond issue price.*

    (a) Compute the selling price of a 12-year, $800,000 bond issue with a contract rate of interest of 10% if the market rate of interest is as follows: (Note: Use the mathematical tables in the text.)

        (1) 10%

        (2) 7%

        (3) 12%

    (b) Prepare the general journal entry to record the sale of the bonds in each situation above.

        (1) Bonds are sold to yield 10%.

JOURNAL

PAGE

	DATE	DESCRIPTION	POST. REF.	DEBIT	CREDIT	
1						1
2						2

        (2) Bonds are sold to yield 7%.

        (3) Bonds are sold to yield 12%.

3. *Accounting for bonds payable.*

Assuming each transaction is independent of the others unless otherwise stated, prepare the following entries, in general journal form, for the Todd Company.

(a) Issued $400,000 of 9%, 10-year bonds at face value plus accrued interest on April 1 (bonds are dated January 1) and pay interest semiannually on January 1 and July 1.

JOURNAL

DATE	DESCRIPTION	POST. REF.	DEBIT	CREDIT

(b) Interest payment on July 1.

(c) What would be the amount of Interest Expense shown on Todd's books after the July 1 payment?

_____

_____

(d) Issued $900,000 of 10%, 8-year bonds at 97 on May 1, 1991, the day the bonds are dated.

(e) Journalize the payment of semiannual interest on the bonds in (d) on November 1 and the accrual of interest on December 31, 1991.

3. *(Cont'd.)*

(f) Journalize the amortization of bond discount on the bonds in (d) on December 31, 1991, using the straight-line method.

(g) On May 1, 1995 (after interest and amortization had been recorded), Todd redeemed $500,000 of the bonds issued in (d) for 101. Journalize the entry to record the bond redemption.

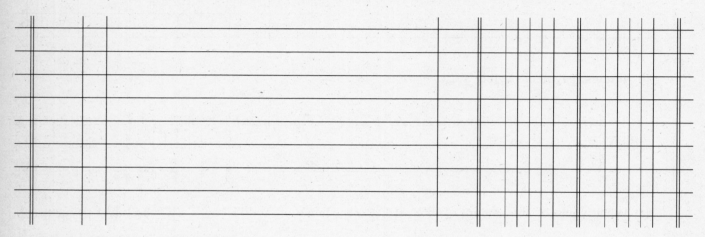

4. *Interest method of amortization.*

On January 1, 1992, the Chavez Container Company issued $800,000 of par value 12%, 10-year bonds for $899,706 (the present value of the bonds assuming a market rate of 10%). The bonds were dated January 1, 1992, and pay interest on June 30 and December 31.

Prepare the journal entries to record the issuance of the bonds and the first two interest payments assuming amortization is recorded on each interest date by the interest method.

JOURNAL

PAGE

DATE		DESCRIPTION	POST. REF.	DEBIT	CREDIT
1992 Jan.	1				
1992 June	30				

4. *(Cont'd.)*

1992 Dec.	31				

5. *Accounting for a bond sinking fund.*

Attie Auto Parts Company issued $900,000 of 12-year bonds on January 1, 1990. The bond indenture provides that a sinking fund be accumulated by 12 annual deposits beginning December 31, 1990. The corporation expects to earn 10% on the fund, requiring the deposit of $42,087 annually.

(a) Give the entry to record the deposit on December 31, 1990.

JOURNAL
PAGE

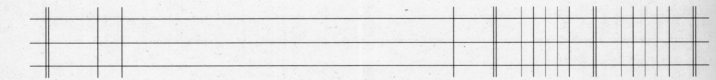

DATE	DESCRIPTION	POST. REF.	DEBIT	CREDIT

(b) Give the entry to record the investment of the entire first deposit in securities on January 2, 1991.

(c) Give the entry to record the 10% income received on December 31, 1991.

(d) The bond indenture for Attie Auto Parts Company also requires the restriction of dividends by equal annual appropriations of retained earnings that are to total the face value of the bonds at maturity. Give the entry to record the appropriation on December 31, 1991.

Chapter 16 (Continued)

5. *(Cont'd.)*

(e) Explain why the annual appropriation differs from the annual deposit in the sinking fund.

_____

_____

_____

_____

_____

_____

_____

_____

_____

_____

_____

(f) On December 31, 2001, Attie Auto Parts Company sells all of its sinking fund investments for $860,000. (Book value is $857,913.) Prepare the entry to record this sale.

(g) Cash available in the sinking fund on December 31, 2001, is composed of the following:

Proceeds from sale of investment	$860,000
Last annual deposit	42,087
Total	$902,087

Prepare the entry to record the payment of the bonds and the transfer of the remaining sinking fund cash to the cash account.

6. *Investment in bonds.*

On July 1, 1990, the day the bonds are dated, the Pedro Corporation purchased $400,000 of the Helms Corporation 10%, 10-year coupon bonds for $453,684, a price to yield 8%. Interest is payable annually on June 30, and amortization is recorded by the interest method. Pedro's fiscal year ends December 31.

Prepare the entries required to record the following transactions on Pedro's books related to the investment.

1990
July 1. Purchase the bonds.

JOURNAL

PAGE

DATE	DESCRIPTION	POST. REF.	DEBIT	CREDIT

Dec. 31. Adjusting entry for accrued interest and amortization.

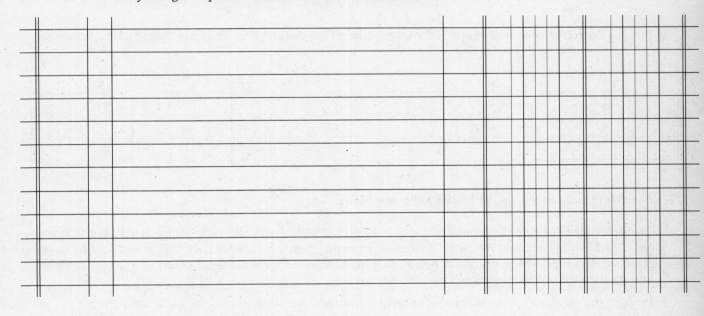

1991
Jan. 1. Reversing entry for interest and amortization.

6. *(Cont'd.)*

1991
June 30. Deposited the coupons for annual interest on the Helms Corporation bonds.

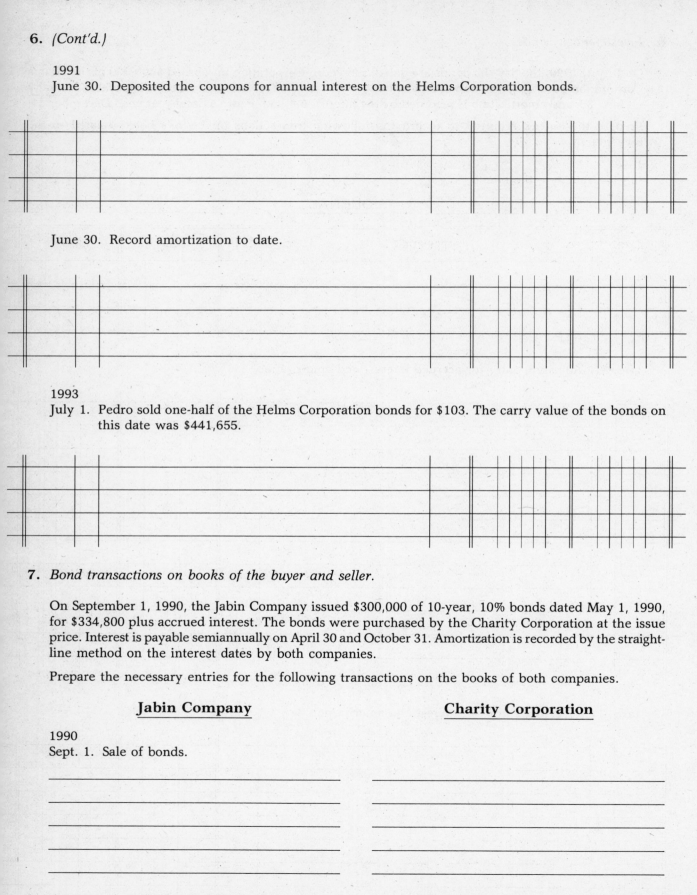

June 30. Record amortization to date.

1993
July 1. Pedro sold one-half of the Helms Corporation bonds for $103. The carry value of the bonds on this date was $441,655.

7. *Bond transactions on books of the buyer and seller.*

On September 1, 1990, the Jabin Company issued $300,000 of 10-year, 10% bonds dated May 1, 1990, for $334,800 plus accrued interest. The bonds were purchased by the Charity Corporation at the issue price. Interest is payable semiannually on April 30 and October 31. Amortization is recorded by the straight-line method on the interest dates by both companies.

Prepare the necessary entries for the following transactions on the books of both companies.

Jabin Company	Charity Corporation

1990
Sept. 1. Sale of bonds.

7. *(Cont'd.)*

Jabin Company	Charity Corporation

1990
Oct. 31. Interest payment and amortization.

_____

Dec. 31. Interest adjustment and amortization.

_____

Dec. 31 Close interest expense and interest income.

_____

1991
Jan. 2. Reversing entry.

_____

Apr. 30. Interest payment and amortization.

_____

7. *(Cont'd.)*

Jabin Company	**Charity Corporation**

1991
Oct. 31. Interest payment and amortization.

_____   _____
_____   _____
_____   _____

Dec. 31. Interest adjustment and amortization.

_____   _____
_____   _____
_____   _____

Dec. 31 Close interest expense and interest income.

_____   _____
_____   _____
_____   _____

1992
May 1. Record purchase and retirement of bonds by Jabin for 101. (Assume interest and amortization were recorded on April 30.)

_____   _____
_____   _____
_____   _____
_____   _____
_____   _____
_____   _____
_____   _____
_____   _____
_____   _____
_____   _____
_____   _____

Notes from lecture and study:

_____

_____

_____

_____

_____

_____

_____

_____

_____

_____

_____

_____

_____

_____

_____

_____

_____

_____

_____

_____

_____

_____

_____

_____

_____

_____

_____

Chapter 17 (Continued)

1. *Cost and equity methods for recording investment in common stock.*

On January 1, 1990, the Shiller Corporation acquired 70,000 shares of common stock (35% of the voting stock) of the Labens Corporation for $190,000.

(a) Record the following transactions on the books of the Shiller Corporation assuming the cost method is used to carry the investment.

   1. Record the investment in the Labens Corporation.
   2. Labens reported a net income of $140,000 for 1990.
   3. Labens paid a $50,000 cash dividend for 1990.
   4. Labens reported a net loss of $20,000 for 1991.

JOURNAL

PAGE

	DATE	DESCRIPTION	POST. REF.	DEBIT	CREDIT	
1						1
2						2
3						3
4						4
5						5
6						6
7						7
8						8
9						9

(b) Record the transactions above on the books of the Shiller Corporation assuming the equity method is used to carry the investment.

JOURNAL

PAGE

	DATE	DESCRIPTION	POST. REF.	DEBIT	CREDIT	
1						1
2						2
3						3
4						4
5						5
6						6
7						7
8						8
9						9
10						10
11						11

2. *Consolidations at acquisition (purchase method).*

The Goldberg Corporation has acquired controlling interest in each of the following corporations. Based on the information given, determine (1) the book equity of investment in each subsidiary, (2) the cost or book equity excess of the investment, and (3) the minority interest in the subsidiary.

(a) Acquired 100% of Hetzel Corporation common stock at a cost of $820,000. The stockholders' equity of Hetzel Corporation was composed of the following at the date of acquisition:

Common stock, $15 par	$450,000	**Answers:**
Premium on common stock	120,000	(1) Book equity of investment in Hetzel Corporation _____
Retained earnings	230,000	

(2) Cost or book equity excess _____

(3) Minority interest _____

(b) Acquired 80% of Vicki Enterprises common stock for $870,000. The stockholders' equity of Vicki Enterprises was composed of the following at the date of acquisition:

Common stock, $6 par	$660,000	**Answers:**
Premium on common stock	150,000	(1) Book equity of investment in Vicki Enterprises _____
Retained earnings	190,000	

(2) Cost or book equity excess _____

(3) Minority interest _____

(c) Acquired 70% of Brian Company common stock for $750,000. The stockholders' equity of Brian Company was composed of the following at the date of acquisition:

Common stock, $4 par	$820,000	**Answers:**
Premium on common stock	140,000	(1) Book equity of investment in Brian Company _____
Retained earnings-deficit	(60,000)	

(2) Cost or book equity excess _____

(3) Minority interest _____

3. *Consolidated work sheet and balance sheet at acquisition (90% ownership).*

The Neal Corporation purchased 90% of the stock of the Sandy Company on July 1, 1990, for $290,000. On this date Sandy owed Neal $5,200 on open account. The balance sheets for the two companies after these transactions on July 1, 1990, appear below.

(a) Complete the consolidated work sheet below.

	Neal Corporation	Sandy Company	Eliminations Debit	Credit	Cons. Bal. Sheet
Assets:					
Cash	$ 26,400	$ 13,600			
Accounts receivable	61,400	32,200			
Merchandise inventory	80,200	62,800			
Investment in Sandy Company	290,000				
Plant and equipment	440,000	236,800			
	$898,000	$345,400			
Liabilities:					
Accounts payable	$ 58,800	$ 23,400			
Capital stock					
Neal	480,000				
Sandy		160,000			
Premium on common stock					
Neal	130,000				
Sandy		80,000			
Retained earnings					
Neal	229,200				
Sandy		82,000			
	$898,000	$345,400			

(b) At the top of the next page, prepare in report form a detailed consolidated balance sheet as of July 1, 1990. The fair value of Sandy's assets are deemed to correspond to their book carrying amounts.

3. *(Cont'd.)*

(b)

_____

_____

_____

_____

_____

_____

_____

_____

_____

_____

_____

_____

_____

_____

_____

_____

_____

_____

_____

(c) Assuming Sandy Company earns net income of $60,000 and pays cash dividends of $20,000 during the fiscal year ending June 30, 1991,

   (1) Prepare the entries, in general journal form, to record the following:

     Neal's share of the earnings.

JOURNAL

PAGE

	DATE	DESCRIPTION	POST. REF.	DEBIT	CREDIT	
1						1
2						2

   The receipt of the cash dividend.

3						3
4						4

3. *(Cont'd.)*

(c) (2) Determine the following as of June 30, 1991:

The balance in Neal's investment account in Sandy.

The amount of minority interest.

4. *Pooling of interest; purchase method.*

On October 1 of the current year, the Ed Corporation issued 80,000 shares of its own $10 par common stock for all of the 80,000 shares of the Midge Company. The fair market value of the Ed stock issued is $20 per share. The balance sheets of the Ed Corporation and the Midge Company on October 1 prior to the acquisition are as follows:

	Ed	Midge
Assets		
Cash	$1,420,000	$ 38,800
Accounts receivable	210,000	64,000
Inventory	600,000	213,200
Plant assets (nets)	2,800,000	920,000
	$5,030,000	$1,236,000
Liabilities and Stockholders' Equity		
Accounts payable	$ 190,000	$ 56,000
Common stock, $10 par	3,200,000	800,000
Premium on common stock	400,000	160,000
Retained earnings	1,240,000	220,000
	$5,030,000	$1,236,000

(a) Prepare the entry on October 1 for Ed Corporation's books assuming the combination is a pooling of interests.

JOURNAL

PAGE

	DATE	DESCRIPTION	POST. REF.	DEBIT	CREDIT	
1						1
2						2
3						3

4. *(Cont'd.)*

(b) Prepare a consolidated balance sheet for the Ed Corporation and the Midge Company as of October 1 assuming the combination is recorded as a pooling of interests.

_____

_____

_____

_____

_____

_____

_____

_____

_____

_____

_____

_____

_____

_____

_____

_____

_____

_____

_____

_____

_____

_____

_____

_____

(c) If the Ed Corporation acquired 100% of the Midge Company stock for cash of $1,200,000, prepare the entry on Ed Corporation's books to record the combination by the purchase method.

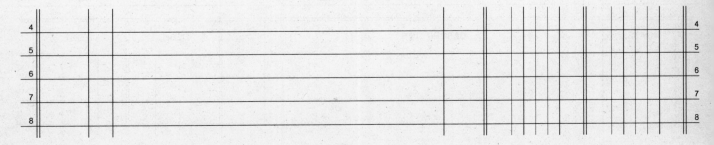

4. *(Cont'd.)*

(d) Prepare a consolidated balance sheet for the Ed Corporation and the Midge Company as of October 1 assuming the combination is recorded as a purchase and that the book values of the net assets of the Midge Company are deemed to represent fair value.

_____

_____

_____

_____

_____

_____

_____

_____

_____

_____

_____

_____

_____

_____

_____

_____

_____

_____

_____

_____

5. *Foreign currency.*

NAPAC, an Atlanta-based corporation, buys and sells merchandise in Switzerland on a regular basis. These transactions are settled in francs (Fr). Prepare the entries, in general journal form, to record the following selected transactions for NAPAC.

(a) Purchased merchandise from Mizelli Supply Co. for 9,800 Fr; exchange rate is .70 Fr per one U.S. dollar.

JOURNAL   PAGE

	DATE	DESCRIPTION	POST. REF.	DEBIT	CREDIT	
1						1
2						2
3						3

5. *(Cont'd.)*

   (b) End of fiscal year (exchange rate is .74 Fr per U.S. dollar). Record end-of-the-year adjustment to payable in (a).

   (c) Paid Mizelli Supply Co. for merchandise purchased in (a); exchange rate is .66 Fr per U.S. dollar.

   (d) NAPAC sold 22,600 Fr of merchandise to Roma Company in Switzerland; exchange rate is .55 Fr per U.S. dollar.

   (e) End of fiscal year (exchange rate is .64 Fr per U.S. dollar). Record adjustment to receivable from Roma Company above.

   (f) Received payment in full from Roma Company; exchange rate is .68 Fr per U.S. dollar.

Chapter 18 STATEMENT OF CASH FLOWS

Notes from lecture and study:

1. *Cash flows from current accounts.*

Indicate how the change in each of the following current assets or current liabilities would affect "cash flows from operating activities." (increase, decrease, or no effect)

Accounts	December 31 19X1	19X2	Increase (Decrease)	Effect
1. Accounts receivable (net)	43,600	51,200	7,600	_____
2. Notes receivable (short-term, from customers)	20,000	8,000	(12,000)	_____
3. Merchandise inventory	121,600	105,600	(16,000)	_____
4. Prepaid advertising	5,400	2,200	(3,200)	_____
5. Accounts payable	34,000	49,000	15,000	_____
6. Salaries payable	11,800	10,400	(1,400)	_____
7. Income taxes payable	4,800	7,300	2,500	_____
8. Cash dividends payable	4,000	9,600	5,600	_____

2. *The effects of transactions on cash flow.*

Indicate how each of the following transactions will affect cash flow and the dollar amount of each. If the item is a use of cash, put parentheses around the amount. If the transaction has no effect, place an "N" in the space.

	Cash
(0) Purchased machinery for cash, $7,800.	(7,800)
(a) Collection of accounts receivable, $6,100.	_____
(b) Borrowing money on short-term note payable, $2,500.	_____
(c) Sold long-term investments carried on books at $9,800 for $13,000, receiving $10,000 cash and a short-term note receivable for the balance.	_____
(d) Declaration of a cash dividend, $18,000.	_____
(e) Payment of note in (b) plus $200 interest.	_____
(f) Furniture costing $16,000 with a book value of $11,400 is sold for $9,500.	_____
(g) Issued 20,000 shares of $5 par common stock for building, $70,000, and equipment, $40,000.	_____
(h) Sale of marketable securities that cost $3,300 for $4,600.	_____
(i) Sold land that cost $22,000 for $37,500 cash.	_____
(j) Payment of dividend in (d).	_____
(k) Sold $150,000 par value bonds at a premium of $13,500.	_____
(l) Purchased treasury stock (common) for $5,400 cash.	_____
(m) Received subscriptions for 6,000 shares of $5 par common stock at $9 per share.	_____
(n) Sale of patent with a book value of $19,400 for cash, $23,700.	_____

Chapter 18 (Continued)

3. *Cash flows from operating activities.*

Net changes in current asset and current liability accounts for the Cricket Corporation for 19X0 were as follows:

	NET CHANGE	
	Dr.	**Cr.**
Cash..		$ 2,600
Accounts receivable..............................	$ 6,100	
Merchandise inventory		4,200
Accrued expenses (operating)	540	
Accounts payable................................		1,700
Income taxes payable		1,940
Dividends payable (cash)	1,500	
	$ 8,140	$10,440
Net decrease in working capital....................	2,300	
	$10,440	$10,440

The Cricket Corporation earned a net income of $38,600 during 19X0. The depreciation expense for the year was $8,400, and amortization of patents was $2,700. Prepare the **cash flows from operating activities** section of a statement of cash flows.

4. *Statement of cash flows.*

Sweet Baby Diapers
Comparative Balance Sheet
December 31, 19X9 and 19X8

	19X9	19X8	Net Change Dr.	Cr.
Cash......................................	$ 32,000	$ 17,000	$15,000	
Accounts receivable (net)	18,000	33,000		$15,000
Merchandise inventory	145,000	120,000	25,000	
Prepaid expenses	5,000	4,000	1,000	
Machinery.................................	140,000	120,000	20,000	
Accumulated depreciation—machinery	(18,000)	(7,000)		11,000
Patent	12,000	0	12,000	
Total assets	$334,000	$287,000		
Accounts payable	$ 32,000	$ 53,000	21,000	
Rent payable...............................	12,000	9,000		3,000
Long-term notes payable....................	70,000	53,000		17,000
Common stock, $10 par	160,000	130,000		30,000
Premium on common stock	45,000	30,000		15,000
Retained earnings..........................	15,000	12,000		3,000
	$334,000	$287,000	$94,000	$94,000

The following information was also obtained from the financial records of Sweet Baby Diapers.

(a) Net income for the year was $9,000.
(b) Depreciation expense was $11,000.
(c) 2,000 shares of common stock were sold for $30,000 cash.
(d) A patent with a fair market value of $15,000 was acquired for 1,000 shares of common stock.
(e) Amortization of the patent was $3,000.
(f) Cash dividends of $6,000 were paid.
(g) A long-term note payable for $8,000 was paid in cash.
(h) A long-term note payable for $25,000 was issued for cash.
(i) Machinery with a cost of $20,000 was purchased for cash.

Required: Prepare a statement of cash flows.

4. *(Cont'd.)*

5. *Statement of cash flows.*

The condensed comparative balance sheet of the Pat Cross Corporation for 19X1 and 19X2 appears below. The ledger sheets for the noncurrent accounts that changed during the year are also presented.

Assets	19X2	19X1
Cash	$ 32,300	$ 9,200
Trade receivables (net)	19,600	16,500
Merchandise inventory	72,890	61,200
Prepaid expenses	7,800	3,300
Land	82,000	62,000
Building	180,000	180,000
Accumulated depreciation—building...........	(54,000)	(45,000)
Equipment	170,000	95,000
Accumulated depreciation—equipment	(38,000)	(31,500)
	$472,590	$350,700

Liabilities & Stockholders' Equity	19X2	19X1
Salaries payable	$ 4,340	$ 1,950
Accounts payable............................	16,260	14,300
Taxes payable	4,000	2,800
Mortgage payable—19X9	75,000	—0—
Common stock, $10 par	220,000	200,000
Premium on common stock	48,000	40,000
Retained earnings	104,990	91,650
	$472,590	$350,700

ACCOUNT **Land**   ACCOUNT NO.

DATE		ITEM	POST. REF.	DEBIT	CREDIT	BALANCE DEBIT	BALANCE CREDIT
19X2 Jan.	1	Balance				62000 00	
June	4	Purchased for cash		20000 00		82000 00	

ACCOUNT **Accumulated Depreciation—Building**   ACCOUNT NO.

DATE		ITEM	POST. REF.	DEBIT	CREDIT	BALANCE DEBIT	BALANCE CREDIT
19X2 Jan.	1	Balance					45000 00
Dec.	31	Depreciation for year			9000 00		54000 00

ACCOUNT **Equipment**   ACCOUNT NO.

DATE		ITEM	POST. REF.	DEBIT	CREDIT	BALANCE DEBIT	BALANCE CREDIT
19X2 Jan.	1	Balance				95000 00	
Oct.	1	Purchased with mortgage		75000 00		170000 00	

5. *(Cont'd.)*

ACCOUNT **Accumulated Depreciation—Equipment**   ACCOUNT NO.

DATE		ITEM	POST. REF.	DEBIT	CREDIT	BALANCE DEBIT	BALANCE CREDIT
19X2 Jan.	1	Balance					3 1 5 0 0 00
Dec.	31	Depreciation for year			6 5 0 0 00		3 8 0 0 0 00

ACCOUNT **Mortgage Payable—19X9**   ACCOUNT NO.

DATE		ITEM	POST. REF.	DEBIT	CREDIT	BALANCE DEBIT	BALANCE CREDIT
19X2 Oct.	1	Assumed in acquiring equipment			7 5 0 0 0 00		7 5 0 0 0 00

ACCOUNT **Common Stock, $10 par**   ACCOUNT NO.

DATE		ITEM	POST. REF.	DEBIT	CREDIT	BALANCE DEBIT	BALANCE CREDIT
19X2 Jan.	1	Balance					20 0 0 0 0 00
Dec.	1	Issued 2,000 shares at $14 per share for cash			2 0 0 0 0 00		22 0 0 0 0 00

ACCOUNT **Premium on Common Stock**   ACCOUNT NO.

DATE		ITEM	POST. REF.	DEBIT	CREDIT	BALANCE DEBIT	BALANCE CREDIT
19X2 Jan.	1	Balance					4 0 0 0 00
Dec.	1	Issued common stock for cash			8 0 0 0 00		4 8 0 0 0 00

ACCOUNT **Retained Earnings**   ACCOUNT NO.

DATE		ITEM	POST. REF.	DEBIT	CREDIT	BALANCE DEBIT	BALANCE CREDIT
19X2 Jan.	1	Balance					9 1 6 5 0 00
Dec.	31	Net income			2 5 3 4 0 00		11 6 9 9 0 00
Dec.	31	Cash dividend paid		1 2 0 0 0 00			10 4 9 9 0 00

5. *(Cont'd.)*

Required: Prepare a statement of cash flows for the Pat Cross Corporation.

6. *Statement of cash flows.*

Comparative balance sheets for the Geneva Corporation for 19X0 and 19X1 are presented below.

	19X0	19X1
Cash	$ 8,000	$ 19,000
Marketable securities	6,500	8,200
Notes receivable (trade)	10,000	4,000
Accounts receivable	22,700	24,200
Merchandise inventory	122,800	126,250
Prepaid expenses	2,000	1,600
Building and equipment	340,000	355,000
Land	45,000	45,000
	$557,000	$583,250
Allowance for bad debts	$ 1,400	$ 1,550
Allowance for depreciation	28,000	44,000
Accounts payable	29,000	26,000
Accrued expenses	1,100	1,400
Income taxes payable	5,000	6,000
Bonds payable	100,000	100,000
Premium on bonds payable	2,500	2,100
Common stock, $10 par	200,000	200,000
Paid-in capital	70,000	70,000
Retained earnings	120,000	132,200
	$557,000	$583,250

Your examination revealed the following additional data:

The income statement for the year was

Sales		$350,000
Cost of merchandise sold		190,000
Gross profit		$160,000
Operating expenses	$ 85,000	
Depreciation	30,000	
Interest expense	5,600	
Loss on sale of equipment	1,200	121,800
Net income before taxes		$ 38,200
Income taxes		14,000
Net income		$ 24,200

During the year, cash dividends of $12,000 were paid by Geneva.

Equipment with a cost of $25,000 and a book value of $11,000 was sold for $9,800. The only other transaction involving the building and equipment was the acquisition of $40,000 of new high-speed equipment.

Required:

(a) Prepare a work sheet for a statement of cash flows for the Geneva Corporation.

(b) Prepare a statement of cash flows for the Geneva Corporation for the year ended 19X1.

6. *(Cont'd.)*

(a)

Geneva Corporation

Work Sheet for Statement of Cash Flows

For Year Ended December 31, 19X1

ACCOUNTS	BALANCE, DEC. 31, 19X0	TRANSACTIONS DEBIT	TRANSACTIONS CREDIT	BALANCE, DEC. 31, 19X1
Cash	8 0 0 0 00			1 9 0 0 0 00
Marketable securities	6 5 0 0 00			8 2 0 0 00
Notes receivable (net)	1 0 0 0 0 00			4 0 0 0 00
Accounts receivable	2 2 7 0 0 00			2 4 2 0 0 00
Merchandise inventory	1 2 2 8 0 0 00			1 2 6 2 5 0 00
Prepaid expenses	2 0 0 0 00			1 6 0 0 00
Building and equipment	3 4 0 0 0 0 00			3 5 5 0 0 0 00
Land	4 5 0 0 0 00			4 5 0 0 0 00
Allowance for bad debts	(1 4 0 0 00)			(1 5 5 0 00)
Allowance for depreciation	(2 8 0 0 0 00)			(4 4 0 0 0 00)
Accounts payable	(2 9 0 0 0 00)			(2 6 0 0 0 00)
Accrued expenses	(1 1 0 0 00)			(1 4 0 0 00)
Income taxes payable	(5 0 0 0 00)			(6 0 0 0 00)
Bonds payable	(1 0 0 0 0 0 00)			(1 0 0 0 0 0 00)
Premium on bonds payable	(2 5 0 0 00)			(2 1 0 0 00)
Common stock	(2 0 0 0 0 0 00)			(2 0 0 0 0 0 00)
Paid-in capital	(7 0 0 0 0 00)			(7 0 0 0 0 00)
Retained earnings	(1 2 0 0 0 0 00)			(1 3 2 2 0 0 00)
Totals	—0—			—0—

6. *(Cont'd.)*

(b)

7. *Direct method of reporting cash flows from operating activities.*

Using the information given in Problem 6 for the Geneva Corporation for 19X0 and 19X1, prepare the cash flows from operating activities section using the direct method.

Calculations:

Chapter 19 FINANCIAL STATEMENT ANALYSIS AND ANNUAL REPORTS

Notes from lecture and study:

_____

_____

_____

_____

_____

_____

_____

_____

_____

_____

_____

_____

_____

_____

_____

_____

_____

_____

_____

_____

_____

_____

_____

_____

_____

_____

_____

1. *Horizontal and vertical analyses.*

A comparative income statement for the Dekker Doll Company for 1991 and 1990 is presented below.

Dekker Doll Company
Comparative Income Statement
For Years Ended December 31, 1991 and 1990

	1991		1990		Increase (Decrease) (A) Amount		(B) Percent		(C) Percent of Sales
Sales	984,000	00	648,600	00					
Sales returns and allowances	24,000	00	8,600	00					
Net sales	960,000	00	640,000	00					
Cost of merchandise sold	450,000	00	364,800	00					
Gross profit	510,000	00	275,200	00					
Selling expenses	130,000	00	76,800	00					
Administrative expenses	84,000	00	51,200	00					
Total operating expenses	214,000	00	128,000	00					
Income before income tax	296,000	00	147,200	00					
Income tax	118,400	00	70,400	00					
Net income	177,600	00	76,800	00					

(a) Complete the horizontal analysis for Dekker by determining the amount of increase or decrease for each item in Column (A) and the percent of increase or decrease for each item in Column (B).

(b) Prepare a vertical analysis of the company's income statement for 1991 in Column (C).

2. *Current position analysis.*

The following balance sheet and income statement data are available for the Orthany Company for the years 1991 and 1990.

	1991	1990
Current assets:		
Cash	$ 7,280	$ 7,600
Marketable securities	5,400	2,800
Accounts receivable (net)	31,600	28,000
Merchandise inventory	32,800	28,200
Prepaid expenses................................	1,800	2,400
Total current assets.............................	$78,880	$69,000
Current liabilities:		
Accounts payable	$14,400	$11,400
Accrued liabilities	4,520	5,300
Notes payable (current)	6,000	—0—
Total current liabilities	$24,920	$16,700

Orthany Company
Income Statement
For Year Ended December 31, 1991

Net sales		$175,400
Cost of merchandise sold:		
Merchandise inventory, January 1	$ 28,200	
Purchases (net)	86,600	
Merchandise available for sale	$114,800	
Merchandise inventory, December 31	32,800	
Cost of merchandise sold		82,000
Gross profit		$ 93,400
Operating expenses		36,480
Net income		$ 56,920

2. *(Cont'd.)*

From the information given, compute the following for 1991:

(a) Working capital.

(b) Current ratio.

(c) Acid-test ratio.

(d) Accounts receivable turnover.

(e) Number of days' sales in receivables. (Use 365 days.)

(f) Merchandise inventory turnover.

(g) Number of days' sales in merchandise inventory.

Chapter 19 (Continued)

3. *Earnings and equities analyses.*

Compute the following analyses for the Hubert Corporation for 1991 using the comparative balance sheet given below. The net sales for 1991 were $1,020,000, and net income after taxes was $107,100. Income taxes were $42,840. The cash dividend paid during 1991 on common stock was $1 per share. The market price of common stock at the end of 1991 was $17 per share.

Hubert Corporation

Comparative Balance Sheet

December 31, 1991 and 1990

	1991	1990
Assets		
Current assets	22 3 9 0 0 00	20 8 0 0 0 00
Investments	11 2 8 0 0 00	8 6 0 0 0 00
Plant assets	60 3 4 0 0 00	53 0 0 0 0 00
Intangible assets	2 2 8 0 0 00	7 0 0 0 0 00
Total assets	96 2 9 0 0 00	89 4 0 0 0 00
Liabilities		
Current liabilities	9 3 6 0 0 00	8 5 4 0 0 00
Bonds payable 10% (issued at par)	20 0 0 0 0 00	20 0 0 0 0 00
Total liabilities	29 3 6 0 0 00	28 5 4 0 0 00
Stockholders' Equity		
Preferred stock 8%, $100 par	8 0 0 0 0 00	8 0 0 0 0 00
Common stock, $5 par	40 0 0 0 0 00	40 0 0 0 0 00
Paid-in capital in excess of par	4 4 0 0 0 00	4 4 0 0 0 00
Retained earnings	14 5 3 0 0 00	8 4 6 0 0 00
Total stockholders' equity	66 9 3 0 0 00	60 8 6 0 0 00
Total liabilities and stockholders' equity	96 2 9 0 0 00	89 4 0 0 0 00

3. *(Cont'd.)*

   (a) Ratio of plant assets to long-term liabilities.

   (b) Ratio of stockholders' equity to liabilities.

   (c) Number of times bond interest charges were earned.

   (d) Ratio of net sales to assets.

   (e) Rate earned on total assets.

   (f) Rate earned on stockholders' equity.

   (g) Rate earned on common stockholders' equity.

   (h) Earnings per share of common stock.

   (i) Price-earnings ratio.

   (j) Dividend yield on common stock.

Chapter 20   MANAGERIAL ACCOUNTING CONCEPTS AND PRINCIPLES

Notes from lecture and study:

_____

_____

_____

_____

_____

_____

_____

_____

_____

_____

_____

_____

_____

_____

_____

_____

_____

_____

_____

_____

_____

_____

_____

1. *Computation of cost of goods manufactured.*

You have assembled the following information concerning the manufacturing activities of the Keller Company for the month of July of the current year.

Direct labor	$182,800
Direct materials inventory, July 1	107,600
Direct materials inventory, July 31	110,400
Direct materials purchases	95,400
Factory overhead	109,680
Work in process inventory, July 1	63,800
Work in process inventory, July 31	57,600

(a) Compute the cost of materials placed in production during July.

(b) Compute the cost of goods manufactured during July.

2. *Computation of cost of goods sold and net income.*

The following information was taken from the adjusted trial balance of Bush Electrical Motors on December 31 of the current year.

Cost of Goods Manufactured	$ 645,440
Finished Goods Inventory, January 1	109,480
Finished Goods Inventory, December 31	114,360
Administrative Expenses	55,280
Sales	1,022,200
Sales Returns and Allowances	19,900
Selling Expenses	122,180

Chapter 20 (Continued)

2. *(Cont'd.)*

(a) Determine cost of goods sold for the year for Bush Electrical Motors.

(b) Determine net income for the year for Bush Electrical Motors.

3. *Statement of cost of goods manufactured and income statement.*

Below you are given selected balances from the ledger accounts of the Jetta Manufacturing Company for the year ended November 30, 19X2.

Direct Materials Inventory, December 1, 19X1	$ 67,600
Work in Process Inventory, December 1, 19X1	96,200
Finished Goods Inventory, December 1, 19X1	79,520
Direct Materials Purchases	561,600
Direct Labor	356,000
Factory Overhead	249,200
Sales	1,809,200
Selling Expenses	178,400
Administrative Expenses	117,080
Direct Materials Inventory, November 30, 19X2	70,800
Work in Process Inventory, November 30, 19X2	103,860
Finished Goods Inventory, November 30, 19X2	75,000
Income Tax Expense	150,800

3. *(Cont'd.)*

(a) Prepare a statement of cost of goods manufactured for the Jetta Manufacturing Company for the year ended November 30, 19X2.

3. *(Cont'd.)*

(b) Prepare an income statement for the Jetta Manufacturing Company for the year ended November 30, 19X2.

4. *Definitions of managerial accounting terms.*

In the left column is a list of terms used in managerial accounting. In the right column are definitions or statements describing these terms. Determine the definition or statement describing each term, and write the identifying letter in the space provided.

Terms	Definition or Statement	Answer

Terms

A. Accuracy
B. Clarity
C. Control
D. Controllable Costs
E. Conversion Costs
F. Differential Cost
G. Direct Cost
H. Direct Labor Cost
I. Direct Materials Cost
J. Discretionary Cost
K. Factory Overhead Cost
L. Fixed Cost
M. Indirect Costs
N. Managerial Accounting
O. Noncontrollable Costs
P. Nonmanufacturing Costs
Q. Opportunity Cost
R. Period Costs
S. Planning
T. Prime Costs
U. Product Costs
V. Relevance
W. Sunk Costs
X. Timeliness
Y. Variable Cost
Z. Work in Process
Inventory

Definition or Statement

1. Data that management uses in conducting daily operations and planning future operations.

2. Setting goals for the use of an organization's resources and developing ways to achieve these goals.

3. Directing operations to achieve the organization's goals and plans.

4. Economic information reported must be pertinent to the specific action being considered by management.

5. The need for accounting reports to contain the most up-to-date information.

6. The need for accounting reports to be correct within the constraints of the use of the report and the inherent inaccuracies in the measurement process.

7. The need for accounting reports to be clear and understandable in both format and content.

8. The cost of materials entering directly into the manufactured product.

9. The cost of wages paid to employees directly involved in changing direct materials into a finished product.

10. Costs other than direct materials cost and direct labor cost incurred in the manufacturing process.

11. The combination of direct materials and direct labor costs.

12. The combination of direct labor and factory overhead costs.

13. The combination of selling and administrative costs.

14. The combination of direct materials, direct labor, and factory overhead.

15. The combination of direct materials costs, direct labor costs, and factory overhead costs that have entered into the manufacturing process but are associated with products that have not been finished.

16. Varies in total dollar amount as the level of activity changes.

Answer

1. _____
2. _____
3. _____
4. _____
5. _____
6. _____
7. _____
8. _____
9. _____
10. _____
11. _____
12. _____
13. _____
14. _____
15. _____
16. _____

4. *(Cont'd.)*

Terms	Definition or Statement	Answer
	17. Remains constant in total dollar amount as the level of activity changes.	17. _____
A. Accuracy		
B. Clarity	18. A cost that can be traced directly to a unit within the enterprise.	18. _____
C. Control		
D. Controllable Costs	19. Costs that cannot be traced directly to a specific unit in the enterprise.	19. _____
E. Conversion Costs		
F. Differential Cost		
G. Direct Cost	20. Costs that a specific level of management can control directly.	20. _____
H. Direct Labor Cost		
I. Direct Materials Cost	21. Costs that another level of management controls.	21. _____
J. Discretionary Cost		
K. Factory Overhead Cost	22. The increase or decrease in cost that is expected from a particular course of action as compared with an alternative course of action.	22. _____
L. Fixed Cost		
M. Indirect Costs		
N. Managerial Accounting		
O. Noncontrollable Costs	23. A cost that is not essential to short-term operations.	23. _____
P. Nonmanufacturing Costs		
Q. Opportunity Cost	24. Costs that have been incurred and cannot be reversed by subsequent decisions.	24. _____
R. Period Costs		
S. Planning		
T. Prime Costs	25. The amount of income that is forgone by selecting one alternative over another.	25. _____
U. Product Costs		
V. Relevance		
W. Sunk Costs	26. Costs that are used up in generating revenue during the current period and that are not involved in the manufacturing process.	26. _____
X. Timeliness		
Y. Variable Cost		
Z. Work in Process Inventory		

Notes from lecture and study:

_____

_____

_____

_____

_____

_____

_____

_____

_____

_____

_____

_____

_____

_____

_____

_____

_____

_____

_____

_____

_____

_____

_____

_____

_____

_____

_____

1. *Statement of cost of goods manufactured, adjusting and closing entries.*

The ledger accounts for Manufacturing Summary and Income Summary for the Berry Manufacturing Co. are presented below.

Manufacturing Summary

19X1			19X1		
Dec. 31	Work in process inventory, Jan. 1	107,000	Dec. 31	Work in process inventory, Dec. 31	94,300
31	Direct materials inventory, Jan. 1	76,000	31	Direct materials inventory, Dec. 31	82,800
31	Direct materials purchases	227,000	31	To Income Summary	597,460
31	Direct labor	196,000			
31	Factory overhead	168,560			
		774,560			774,560

Income Summary

19X1			19X1		
Dec. 31	Finished goods inventory, Jan. 1	153,000	Dec. 31	Finished goods inventory, Dec. 31	162,000
31	From Manufacturing Summary	597,460			

(a) Prepare a statement of cost of goods manufactured for the Berry Manufacturing Co. for the year ended December 31, 19X1.

1. *(Cont'd.)*

(b) Prepare the general journal entries to adjust the three inventory accounts on December 31, 19X1, for the Berry Manufacturing Co.

JOURNAL

	DATE		DESCRIPTION	POST. REF.	DEBIT	CREDIT	
1							1
2							2
3							3
4							4
5							5
6							6
7							7
8							8
9							9
10							10
11							11
12							12
13							13
14							14
15							15
16							16
17							17

(c) Prepare the general journal entries to close all temporary manufacturing accounts and the manufacturing summary account.

18							18
19							19
20							20
21							21
22							22
23							23
24							24
25							25
26							26
27							27

Chapter 21 (Continued)

1. *(Cont'd.)*

(d) Compute the overhead rate for the Berry Manufacturing Co. for the year.

_____

(e) If the work in process inventory December 31 has $30,000 in direct labor, how much factory overhead and how much direct material cost are in this inventory?

1. Factory overhead _____

2. Direct material _____

2. *Job order flows with journal entries.*

Prepare the entries, in general journal form, to record the following transactions completed by the Minta Manufacturing Company during the month of May.

(a) Purchased material on account, $178,600.

JOURNAL

PAGE

	DATE		DESCRIPTION	POST. REF.	DEBIT	CREDIT	
1							1
2							2

(b) Materials requisitioned as follows:

For specific jobs	$109,300
For general factory use	16,100

3				3
4				4
5				5

(c) Labor charged during period:

Direct	$160,000
Indirect	41,300

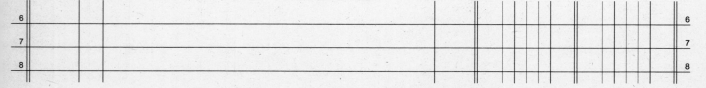

6				6
7				7
8				8

2. *(Cont'd.)*

(d) Factory overhead is applied at the predetermined rate of 80% of direct labor cost.

(e) Jobs completed during period totaled $342,000.

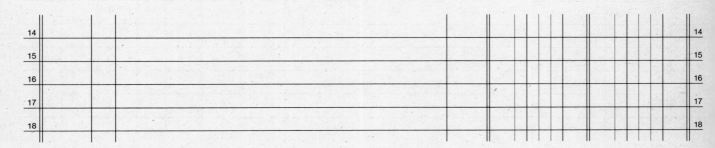

(f) Sales during month on account, $760,000; cost, $372,000.

(g) Selling and administrative expenses during period paid in cash $143,800.

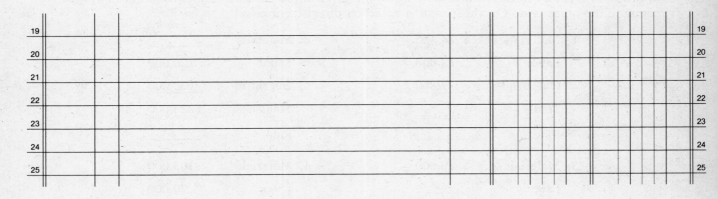

2. *(Cont'd.)*

(h) Prepare the income statement for the Minta Manufacturing Company for the month of May. (The company's fiscal year ends July 31, and factory overhead is not closed until that time.)

_____

3. *Relationship of the elements of work in process and the overhead rate.*

In each numbered exercise below, there are five elements of data (materials, labor, overhead, total work in process inventory, and overhead rate). You are given three of these elements and are required to compute the other two. (Overhead rate is based on direct labor cost.)

1.	Materials	$ 24,400		2.	Materials	$_____
	Labor	13,000			Labor	120,000
	Overhead	7,800			Overhead	30,000
	Total	$_____			Total	$223,000
	Rate	_____			Rate	_____

3.	Materials	$ 19,500		4.	Materials	$103,000
	Labor	_____			Labor	70,000
	Overhead	_____			Overhead	_____
	Total	$112,000			Total	$222,000
	Rate	85%			Rate	_____

5.	Materials	$ 40,200
	Labor	_____
	Overhead	31,000
	Total	$_____
	Rate	80%

4. *Job order illustrated with subsidiary ledgers.*

The following general and subsidiary ledger account balances are given for the Jabin Manufacturing Company as of November 30. The company's fiscal year ends December 31. The company uses a job order cost accounting system and keeps its finished goods inventory on a first-in, first-out basis.

GENERAL LEDGER

Cash	
9,660	

Accounts Receivable	
45,400	

Finished Goods	
58,240	

Work in Process	
15,960	

Materials	
30,790	

Plant and Equipment	
956,000	

Accumulated Depreciation	
	203,400

Accounts Payable	
	28,600

Wages Payable	
	15,200

Common Stock, $5 par	
	400,000

Retained Earnings	
	44,950

Sales	
	1,417,000

Cost of Goods Sold	
702,900	

Selling and Administrative Expenses	
297,400	

Factory Overhead	
Actual	Applied
181,100	188,300

4. *(Cont'd.)*

SUBSIDIARY LEDGERS

MATERIALS LEDGER	WORK IN PROCESS (JOB) LEDGER

Material CHI

Bal.	10,200		

Material PHI

Bal.	12,370		

Material THI

Bal.	8,220		

No. 605

Bal.	6,500		

No. 606

Bal.	5,520		

No. 607

Bal.	3,940		

FINISHED GOODS LEDGER	FACTORY OVERHEAD LEDGER— ACTUAL

Product BETA

11,300 @ 2.20	24,860		

Product GAMMA

20,800 @ 1.10	22,880		

Product SIGMA

14,000 @ .75	10,500		

Supplies

26,800	

Maintenance

99,700	

Depreciation

54,600	

4. *(Cont'd.)*

(a) Prepare a trial balance for the Jabin Manufacturing Company as of November 30, 19--. Also prepare a schedule of subsidiaries for the three inventory accounts and Factory Overhead.

Chapter 21 (Continued)

4. *(Cont'd.)*

(b) Prepare journal entries for the Jabin Manufacturing Company for the following transactions occurring in December, and post to the general ledger and subsidiary accounts. Use the transaction number as the posting reference.

(1) Materials purchased on account were received.

Material Chi	$32,400
Material Phi.......................................	15,600
Material Thi.......................................	4,440

JOURNAL PAGE

	DATE		DESCRIPTION	POST: REF.	DEBIT	CREDIT	
1							1
2							2
3							3

(2) Materials requisitions for December are summarized as follows:

Req. No.	Material	Amount	Job	Overhead Subsidiary
1294	Chi	15,980	605	
1295	Chi	11,840	606	
	Phi	6,400	606	
1296	Thi	3,940	—	Supplies
1297	Phi	8,600	607	

(3) The following time tickets were verified for the month.

Ticket No.	Amount	Job	Overhead Subsidiary
721	8,100	605	
722	12,400	606	
723	10,100		Maintenance
724	3,600	606	
725	9,500	605	
726	6,200	607	

4. *(Cont'd.)*

(b) (4) Factory overhead was charged to the jobs. The company is using a 70% predetermined overhead rate based on the direct labor cost.

(5) Depreciation of factory equipment of $6,100 is charged for December.

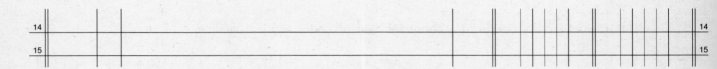

(6) Job No. 605 and No. 606 were completed during December. Job No. 605 produced 20,000 units of Product Beta; Job No. 606 produced 36,400 units of Product Gamma.

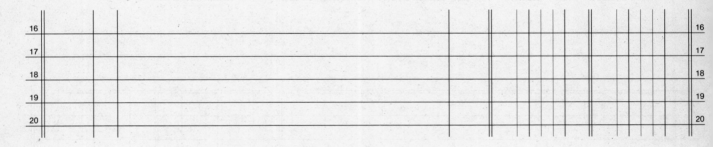

(7) Sales on account: 21,300 of Product Beta, selling price $3.50 per unit; 32,800 of Product Gamma, selling price $2.50 per unit; 8,000 of Product Sigma, selling price $1.65 per unit.

(8) Collection on accounts receivable, $147,400.

Chapter 21 (Continued)

4. *(Cont'd.)*

(b) (9) Selling and administrative expenses paid, $58,750.

(10) Accounts payable paid, $51,200; wages paid, $37,400.

(11) Closed factory overhead account for over or under applied balance.

(c) Prepare a trial balance for the Jabin Manufacturing Company as of December 31, 19--.

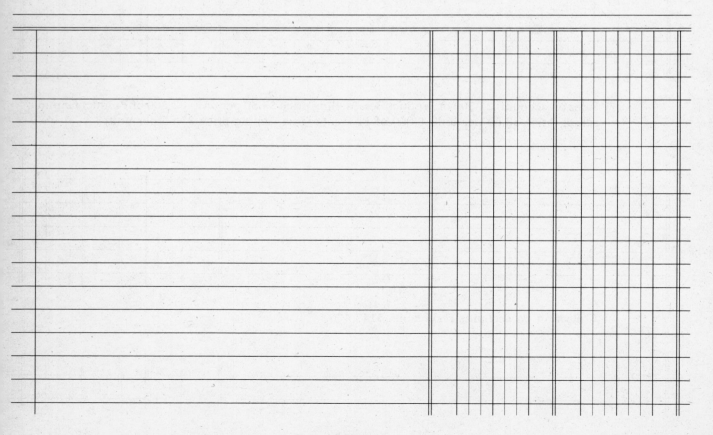

4. *(Cont'd.)*

(d) Prove the subsidiary ledgers with the control accounts for inventories.

Prepare an income statement for the year ended December 31 for the Jabin Manufacturing Company.

Notes from lecture and study:

_____

_____

_____

_____

_____

_____

_____

_____

_____

_____

_____

_____

_____

_____

_____

_____

_____

_____

_____

_____

_____

_____

_____

_____

_____

_____

_____

1. *Computing equivalent units of production.*

   Compute the equivalent units of production for each of the following situations in Mining Department 4.

   (a) No beginning inventory in the department; 9,600 units are placed in process; all are 1/3 completed at the end of the month.

   _____

   _____

   _____

   _____

   _____

   (b) No beginning inventory; 5,400 units are placed in process; 1,200 units are still in the department at the end of the month, 3/4 completed.

   _____

   _____

   _____

   _____

   _____

   _____

   (c) There were 3,600 units in the beginning inventory, 1/2 completed; 10,000 units were placed in process during the month; 2,700 units remain in the ending inventory, 2/3 completed.

   _____

   _____

   _____

   _____

   _____

   _____

   (d) There were 15,000 units in the beginning inventory, 60% completed; 12,000 units are placed in process during the period; 4,400 units remain in the ending inventory, 40% completed.

   _____

   _____

   _____

   _____

   _____

   _____

Chapter 22 (Continued)

2. *Preparing a quantity schedule and computing EUP.*

Selected information concerning production in the Finishing Department for September is presented in the following ledger account. All materials are placed in process at the beginning of production.

ACCOUNT **Work in Process—Finishing Department**   ACCOUNT NO.

DATE		ITEM	POST. REF.	DEBIT	CREDIT	BALANCE DEBIT	BALANCE CREDIT
Sept.	1	Bal., 3,600 units, 1/3 comp.		16 800 00		16 800 00	
	30	Spraying Dept., 27,600					
		units at $12		331 200 00		348 000 00	
	30	Direct labor		90 000 00		438 000 00	
	30	Factory overhead		60 000 00		498 000 00	
	30	Goods finished, 24,800					
		Bal., 6,400 units, 3/4 comp.					

(a) Prepare the quantity section of the cost of production report for the Finishing Department for September.

_____

_____

_____

_____

_____

_____

_____

_____

_____

_____

_____

_____

(b) Determine the equivalent units of production for the month.

_____

_____

_____

_____

_____

_____

_____

_____

_____

2. *(Cont'd.)*

(c) What is the processing cost per equivalent unit in the Finishing Department for September?

_____

_____

_____

_____

_____

_____

_____

(d) Determine the cost of goods finished during September.

_____

_____

_____

_____

_____

_____

_____

_____

_____

_____

_____

_____

_____

(e) Determine the cost of the 6,400 units in the Finishing Department at the end of September.

_____

_____

_____

_____

_____

_____

_____

_____

3. *Journal entries for process cost flows.*

The Kashif Manufacturing Company has only one processing department. Kashif had the following inventories on February 1 of the current year.

Finished goods (8,200 units @ 21)	$172,200
Work in process (7,000 units, 2/5 completed)	71,600
Materials	32,800

Prepare the entries to record the following transactions completed by the Kashif Manufacturing Company during the month of February.

(a) Purchased material on account, $29,200.

(b) Materials requisitioned as follows:

For processing	$36,380
Indirect materials	2,425

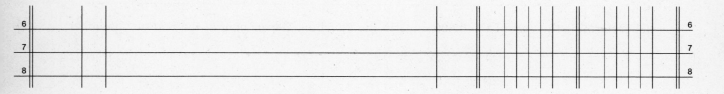

(c) Labor charged during period:

Direct labor	$51,800
Indirect labor	4,760

(d) Factory overhead is applied at the rate of 105% of direct labor cost.

3. *(Cont'd.)*

(e) Production costs of $206,300 transferred from work in process to finished goods represent 8,800 fully processed units, including the beginning inventory. Inventory of work in process on February 28 is 700 units, 1/2 completed.

12							12
13							13
14							14
15							15
16							16
17							17

(f) Sales during month on account, 8,500 units at $75 per unit. (Use first-in, first-out method for recording finished goods.)

18							18
19							19
20							20
21							21
22							22
23							23
24							24
25							25
26							26
27							27
28							28

4. *Joint and by-products.*

Processing Department 71 produces two joint products, P and D, and one by-product, I. Charges and production in Department 71 for the current month are as follows. (There was no inventory in Department 71 at the beginning or end of the month.)

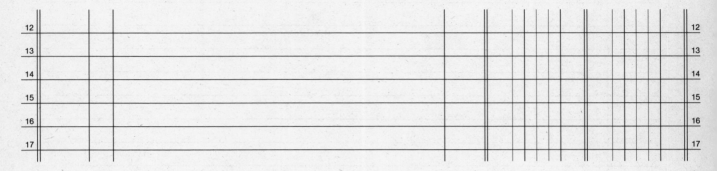

Materials	$ 405,000
Direct labor	430,000
Factory overhead	344,000
	$1,179,000

Production		Sales Prices	
P	140,000 units	P	$10.00
D	80,000 units	D	7.50
I	12,000 units	I	.50

4. *(Cont'd.)*

Determine the allocation of costs to the three products and the unit cost of each.

_____

_____

_____

_____

_____

_____

_____

_____

_____

_____

_____

_____

_____

_____

_____

_____

_____

_____

_____

_____

_____

_____

_____

_____

_____

Notes from lecture and study:

Chapter 23 (Continued)

1. *Mixed cost graphs.*

The Sioux Drilling Company drills gas wells using rented drilling equipment.

Required: Prepare a mixed cost graph in each situation below.

(a) The rental charges are $50,000 per year plus $16 for each hour the equipment is used.

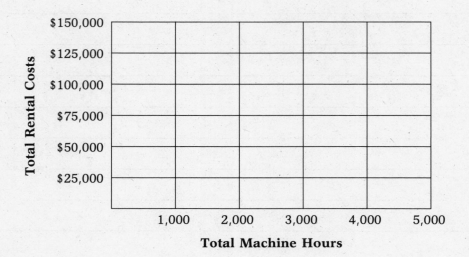

(b) The rental charges are $75,000 per year plus $16 for each machine hour used over 2,000 hours.

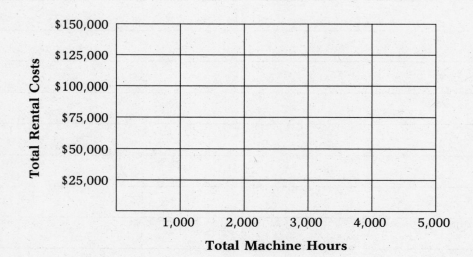

2. *Break-even point and profits.*

Bethany Corporation manufactures clock radios. Bethany estimates fixed costs for 19X1 to be $350,000 and estimated variable costs at $6 per unit. It is estimated that 80,000 radios will be sold in 19X1 for $20 each. Capacity output for Bethany Corporation is 100,000 radios.

Determine the break-even point for Bethany Corportion in terms of the following:

(a) Dollars of sales.

(b) Units.

(c) Capacity.

(d) How many radios will Bethany have to sell to earn a profit of $70,000?

(e) What total dollar sales volume must Bethany have in order to earn a profit of 14% of sales?

3. *Effects of changes in costs on break-even analysis.*

The Leahanne Manufacturing Company manufactures electric perk coffee pots for home use. Leahanne estimates that 300,000 coffee pots will be sold in 19X0 for $15 each. Leahanne estimates fixed costs for 19X0 will be $600,000, and variable costs will be $9 each.

(a) Compute the break-even point in dollars for Leahanne for 19X0.

(b) Leahanne is considering an increase in the base pay for all factory workers, which would increase fixed costs by $90,000. If this raise is given for 19X0, what will the break-even point be in dollars?

(c) Leahanne is also considering an increase in wages by $.40 per hour rather than the base pay increase in (b) above. This raise would increase variable costs to $10.20 per unit and have no effect on fixed costs. Compute the break-even point in dollars if the hourly raise is granted.

4. *Cost-volume-profit chart and profit-volume chart.*

At a sales level of 120,000 units (capacity 160,000 units), budget costs for Horrell Company are as follows:

	Fixed	Variable
Cost of goods sold	$210,000	$400,000
Operating:		
Selling	80,000	260,000
General	40,000	120,000
	$330,000	$780,000

The unit selling price is $10.

(a) Determine the break-even point in dollars of sales for Horrell Company.

(b) Using the form provided, prepare a cost-volume-profit chart for Horrell Company.

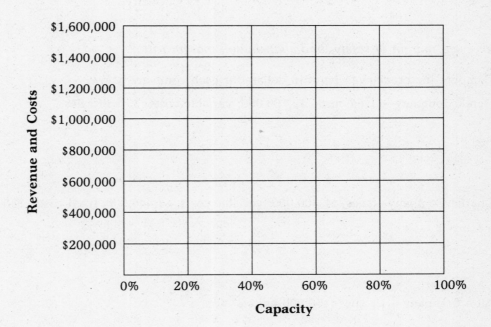

Chapter 23 (Continued)

4. *(Cont'd.)*

(c) Using the form provided, prepare a profit-volume chart.

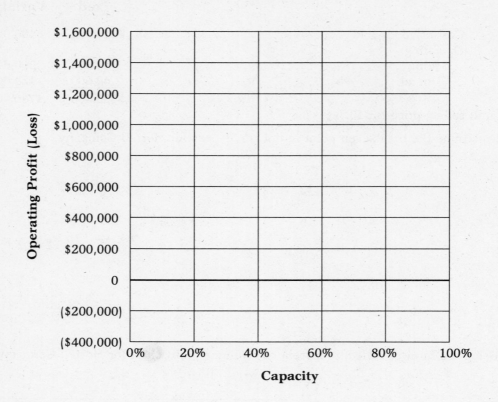

5. *Break even, margin of safety, and contribution margin ratio.*

(a) Compute the break-even point in dollars for each company below.

Derek Company—Fixed costs, $2,100,000; variable costs, 70% of sales.

Charlie Company—Sales, $2,400,000; variable costs, $1,440,000; fixed costs, $800,000.

Attie Company—(1)	Sales (150,000 units at $30)	$4,500,000
	Fixed costs	900,000
	Variable costs ($16.50 per unit)	2,475,000

5. *(Cont'd.)*

(a) (2) How many units will have to be sold for Attie Company to break even?

(3) How many units will have to be sold for Attie Company to earn a profit of $300,000?

(4) What dollar sales volume is required for Attie Company to earn a profit of 25% of sales?

(b) Compute the margin of safety for Charlie Company at the $3,500,000 sales level.

(c) Compute the margin of safety for Attie Company if it sells 125,000 units.

(d) Compute the contribution margin for each company listed.

Derek Company   Charlie Company   Attie Company

Notes from lecture and study:

1. *Income statements using absorption costing and variable costing.*

Berkeley's Truck Radiators began operation in January 1991. During the first year of operation, the company manufactured 40,000 units of which 32,000 were sold at $105 per unit. Variable manufacturing costs were $35 per unit, and fixed factory overhead was $272,000. Variable selling and administrative expenses were $18 per unit, and fixed selling and administrative expenses were $145,000.

(a) Prepare an absorption costing income statement for 1991 for Berkeley's Truck Radiators.

1. *(Cont'd.)*

(b) Prepare a variable costing income statement for 1991 for Berkeley's Truck Radiators.

(c) Explain the reason for the difference in the amount of net income reported in (a) and (b).

2. *Cost of goods manufactured using variable costing and absorption costing.*

On October 31, the end of the first year of operations, Roland Company manufactured 80,000 units and sold 70,000 units. The following income statement was prepared based on the variable costing concept.

Roland Company
Income Statement
For Year Ended October 31, 19--

Sales		$1,900,000
Variable cost of goods sold:		
Variable cost of goods manufactured	$1,120,000	
Less ending inventory	140,000	
Variable cost of goods sold		980,000
Manufacturing margin		$ 920,000
Variable selling and administrative expenses ...		140,000
Contribution margin		$ 780,000
Fixed costs and expenses:		
Fixed manufacturing costs	$ 160,000	
Fixed selling and administrative expenses ...	105,000	
Total fixed costs and expenses		265,000
Income from operations		$515,000

Determine the unit cost of goods manufactured, based on the following:

(a) Variable costing concept.

_____

_____

_____

_____

_____

_____

_____

_____

(b) Absorption costing concept.

_____

_____

_____

_____

_____

_____

_____

_____

3. *Change in sales mix and contribution margin.*

Tofu Luggage Company manufactures luggage, Sets P and Q, and is operating at full capacity. To manufacture Set P requires three times the number of machine hours as required for Set Q. Market research indicates that 3,000 additional Q sets could be sold. The contribution margin by unit of product is as follows:

	Set P	Set Q
Sales price	$60	$48
Variable cost of goods sold	36	30
Manufacturing margin	$24	$18
Variable selling and administrative expenses	13	10
Contribution margin	$11	$ 8

Prepare a tabulation indicating the increase or decrease in total contribution margin if 3,000 additional Q sets are produced and sold.

---

4. *Contribution margin analysis.*

Pedigo Products manufactures folding card tables. The following data for Pedigo for 19X1 are available.

	Actual	Planned	Difference (Increase or Decrease*)
		For Year Ended December 31, 19X1	
Sales	$286,000	$300,000	$14,000*
Less:			
Variable cost of goods sold	$120,250	$120,000	$ 250
Variable selling and administrative			
expenses	63,700	75,000	11,300*
Total	$183,950	$195,000	$11,050*
Contribution margin	$102,050	$105,000	$ 2,950*
Number of units sold	13,000	15,000	
Per unit:			
Sales price	$22.00	$20.00	
Variable cost of goods sold	$ 9.25	$ 8.00	
Variable selling and administrative			
expenses	$ 4.90	$ 5.00	

(a) Prepare a contribution analysis of the sales quantity and price factors.

4. *(Cont'd.)*

    (b) Based upon the previous data for Pedigo Products, prepare a contribution analysis of the variable costs and expenses for the year ended December 31, 19X1.

Notes from lecture and study:

_____

_____

_____

_____

_____

_____

_____

_____

_____

_____

_____

_____

_____

_____

_____

_____

_____

_____

_____

_____

_____

_____

_____

_____

_____

_____

_____

_____

1. *Sales, production, direct materials, and direct labor budgets.*

Crockett Manufacturing Company expects a 20% increase over the 300,000 units of product W sold last year and a 10% increase in the 240,000 units of Product Y sold. Budgeted raw materials and finished goods inventories for the year were as follows:

	Beginning	Ending
Raw Materials		
Goo	42,000 lbs	38,600 lbs
Woo	51,000 gal	53,400 gal
Finished Goods		
W	20,000 units	18,000 units
Y	16,000 units	17,800 units

Materials and labor required in production:

For one unit of W—2 pounds of Goo; 2 gallons of Woo; direct labor, 2 hours at $6 per hour

For one unit of Y—3 pounds of Goo; 2 gallons of Woo; direct labor, 3 hours at $6 per hour

Factory overhead is applied at the rate of $4 per hour of labor used.

Budgeted costs of raw materials:

Goo—$1.60 per pound
Woo—$2.40 per gallon

Selling price of W is $75 and Y is $80.

Prepare the following:

(a) A sales budget in units and dollars.

(b) A production budget in units.

1. *(Cont'd.)*

(c) A direct materials purchases budget for products Goo and Woo.

(d) A direct labor cost budget.

(e) Determine the production cost budgeted *per unit* of W and Y.

Chapter 25 (Continued)

2. *Cash budget.*

The trial balance for the Myku Corporation as of January 1, 19--, the beginning of the company's fiscal year, is shown below.

	Dr.	Cr.
Cash	$ 46,800	
Accounts Receivable	90,000	
Investments	136,000	
Building and Equipment	530,000	
Accounts Payable		$ 76,000
Notes Payable—Bank		40,000
Accrued Expenses		19,200
Capital Stock, $5 par		400,000
Retained Earnings		267,600
	$802,800	$802,800

Budgeted income statements for January and February are as follows:

	January	February
Sales	$386,000	$514,000
Cost of goods sold	220,000	306,000
Gross profit	$166,000	$208,000
Operating expenses	68,000	92,000
Net income	$ 98,000	$116,000

All sales for the Myku Corporation are on account; 70% of these receivables are expected to be collected in the month of sale, the balance in the following month. Monthly depreciation represents $10,000 of the cost of goods sold and $16,000 of operating expenses. Of the remaining costs and expenses, 80% are expected to be paid in the month they are incurred and the balance in the following month. The note payable is due February 15 with interest for three months at 12%. At their annual meeting in late January, the board of directors agreed to declare a cash dividend of $.50 per share in January payable in February. They also decided to purchase equipment in February at a cost of $56,000 with a down payment of 40% and the balance in three equal monthly installments. The investments include Zero Corporation bonds with a face value of $30,000 that mature in early February, plus interest of $3,000. All the accrued expenses are payable in January.

Myku desires to keep a minimum cash balance of $25,000.

Prepare a monthly cash budget for January and February.

2. *(Cont'd.)*

3. *Flexible budget for operating expenses.*

Prepare a flexible operating budget for the Tricia Company for the sales levels indicated below.

Tricia Company
Flexible Operating Expense Budget
For the Month of March 19--

Expense Item	Budget Allowance at Indicated Sales Levels		
	$2,000,000	$2,400,000	$2,800,000
Office salaries $45,000 (not related to sales volume)......................	_____	_____	_____
Sales commissions (8% of sales)	_____	_____	_____
Advertising (basic budget of $50,000 plus 1% of sales).................	_____	_____	_____
Office supplies expense (2% of sales).	_____	_____	_____
Traveling (additional allowance of 2.0% of sales increase).................	35,000	_____	_____
Depreciation and maintenance of sales equipment $56,000 (not related to sales volume)	_____	_____	_____
Miscellaneous expense ($3,000 plus 1/4% of sales)	_____	_____	_____
Total operating expenses	_____	_____	_____

4. *Standard costs and variances.*

The Williford Company manufactures ceiling fans and uses a standard cost system. An analysis of costs shows the direct material used in one fan costing $5.20. One hour of direct labor costs $8 with standard production being two fans per hour. Variable manufacturing overhead is estimated at $2.50 per hour, and fixed overhead is set at $35,000 per year. Normal operating capacity is 70,000 fans per year.

(a) Determine the standard cost per fan based on the above information.

_____

_____

_____

_____

_____

_____

_____

_____

(b) During the year 60,000 fans were produced at the following costs:

Materials (66,000 units)	$330,000
Labor (31,000 hours at $7.80)	241,800
Variable overhead	80,600
Fixed overhead	35,000

Calculate the following variances and indicate whether favorable or unfavorable.

(1) Direct materials cost variance.

Price variance.

_____

_____

_____

_____

_____

Quantity variance.

_____

_____

_____

_____

Total direct materials cost variance.

_____

_____

_____

_____

_____

Chapter 25 (Continued)

4. *(Cont'd.)*

  (b) (2) Direct labor cost variance.

      Time variance.

_____

_____

_____

_____

_____

      Rate variance.

_____

_____

_____

_____

_____

      Total direct labor cost variance.

_____

_____

_____

    (3) Factory overhead cost variance.

      Volume variance.

_____

_____

_____

_____

_____

      Controllable variance.

_____

_____

_____

_____

_____

      Total factory overhead cost variance.

_____

_____

Notes from lecture and study:

Chapter 26 (Continued)

1. *Budget performance report.*

The budget for the Painting and Drying Department of Plant 3 for the current month ended April 30 is shown in the budget performance report form below. During April the actual costs incurred in the Painting and Drying Department were factory wages, $71,600; materials, $30,550; supervisory salaries, $15,200; power and lights, $13,500; depreciation of plant and equipment, $8,400; maintenance, $3,870; insurance and property taxes, $2,160.

(a) Complete the budget performance report for the supervisor of the Painting and Drying Department for the month of April.

Budget Performance Report—Supervisor
Painting and Drying Department—Plant 3
For Month Ended April 30, 19--

	BUDGET	ACTUAL	OVER	UNDER
Factory wages	$ 72 800 00			
Materials	27 400 00			
Supervisory salaries	15 200 00			
Power and light	13 260 00			
Depreciation of plant and equipment	8 400 00			
Maintenance	4 480 00			
Insurance and property taxes	2 160 00			

(b) For what significant variations in costs might the supervisor be expected to request supplemental reports?

_____

_____

_____

_____

2. *Apportionment of operating expenses.*

LPN is a wholesale operation with three departments. The following departmental data is provided for the current year.

Dept.	Sales	Purchases	Average Cost of Equipment	Floor Space	Payroll (Sales)
L	$ 800,000	$ 392,000	$ 240,000	14,400 sq. ft.	$ 40,800
P	1,200,000	448,000	600,000	24,000 sq. ft.	48,400
N	400,000	280,000	160,000	9,600 sq. ft.	30,400
Total	$2,400,000	$1,120,000	$1,000,000	48,000 sq. ft.	$119,600

Determine the departmental allocation of each of the following operating expenses for the year.

Expense	Basis of Allocation	Amount	Department Allocation L	P	N
(a) Advertising	Sales	$ 36,000	_____	_____	_____
(b) Delivery	Sales	12,000	_____	_____	_____
(c) Depreciation	Cost of equipment	60,000	_____	_____	_____
(d) Insurance on equipment	Cost of equipment	4,500	_____	_____	_____
(e) Office salaries	Sales	54,000	_____	_____	_____
(f) Property tax	Cost of equipment	6,600	_____	_____	_____
(g) Rent	Floor space	96,000	_____	_____	_____
(h) Sales salaries	Payroll	119,600	_____	_____	_____
(i) Supplies	Purchases	5,800	_____	_____	_____
(j) Uncollectible accounts	Sales	15,000	_____	_____	_____
(k) Utilities	Floor space	27,000	_____	_____	_____

3. *Income statement—departmental margin approach.*

Yamaguchi Wine and Cheese is organized with two departments—Department W, Wine, and Department C, Cheese. The following income statement information is available for Yamaguchi for the year ended December 31.

Net sales—Department W	$810,000
Net sales—Department C	550,000
Cost of goods sold—Department W	386,000
Cost of goods sold—Department C	278,000

Direct Departmental Expenses:

Sales salaries expense—Department W	68,800
Sales salaries expense—Department C	57,200
Property tax—Department W	3,240
Property tax—Department C	2,680
Uncollectible accounts expense (½ of 1% of sales)	
Depreciation expense, equipment—Department W	5,300
Depreciation expense, equipment—Department C	3,600
Store supplies—Department W	1,300
Store supplies—Department C	1,050

Indirect Expenses:

Office salaries expense	64,600
Rent expense	48,000
Utilities expense	33,480
Advertising expense	19,600
Miscellaneous expense	8,400

Using the form provided on the following page, prepare an income statement departmentalized through departmental margin.

3. *(Cont'd.)*

Yamaguchi Wine and Cheese

Income Statement

For Year Ended December 31, 19—

	DEPARTMENT W		DEPARTMENT C		TOTAL	
Net sales						
Cost of goods sold						
Gross profit						
Direct departmental expenses:						
Sales salaries expense						
Property tax expense						
Uncollectible accounts expense						
Depreciation expense						
Store supplies expense						
Total direct departmental expenses						
Departmental margin						
Indirect expenses:						
Office salaries expense						
Rent expense						
Utilities expense						
Advertising expense						
Miscellaneous expense						
Total indirect expenses						
Net income						

4. *Income statement departmentalized through income from operations.*

R-Barret Shirts and Ties is a specialty shop operating two sales departments—Department S, Shirts, and Department T, Ties. The trial balance shown on the following page was prepared as of June 30, the end of the current fiscal year, after all adjustments, including those for inventories, were recorded and posted.

Inventories at the beginning of the year were as follows: Department S, $112,400; Department T, $35,200. The bases to be used in apportioning expenses, together with other essential information, are as follows:

Sales salaries—payroll records: Department S, $34,400; Department T, $23,600.

Advertising expense—usage: Department S, $9,400; Department T, $6,200.

Depreciation expense—average cost of equipment. Equipment balances at beginning of year: Department S, $42,000; Department T, $26,000. Equipment balances at end of year: Department S, $38,000; Department T, $34,000.

Store supplies expense—requisitions: Department S, $805; Department T, $690.

Office salaries—Department S, 60%; Department T, 40%.

Rent expense and heating and lighting expense—floor space: Department S, 1,800 square feet; Department T, 600 square feet.

Property tax expense and insurance expense—average cost of equipment plus average cost of inventories.

Uncollectible accounts expense, miscellaneous selling expense, and miscellaneous general expense—volume of gross sales.

4. *(Cont'd.)*

R-Barret Shirts and Ties
Trial Balance
June 30, 19--

Cash	33,400	
Accounts Receivable	55,100	
Inventories—Department S	107,600	
Inventories—Department T	39,800	
Prepaid Insurance	3,400	
Store Supplies	715	
Store Equipment	72,000	
Accumulated Depreciation—Store Equipment		26,400
Accounts Payable		17,600
Common Stock		130,000
Retained Earnings		64,640
Income Summary	151,600	127,510
Sales—Department S		390,000
Sales—Department T		130,000
Sales Returns and Allowances—Department S	5,200	
Sales Returns and Allowances—Department T	3,800	
Purchases—Department S	115,400	
Purchases—Department T	62,200	
Sales Salaries	58,000	
Advertising Expense	15,600	
Depreciation Expense—Store Equipment	11,900	
Store Supplies Expense	1,495	
Miscellaneous Selling Expense	480	
Office Salaries	36,400	
Rent Expense	24,000	
Heating and Lighting Expense	15,400	
Property Tax Expense	12,400	
Insurance Expense	4,700	
Uncollectible Accounts Expense	2,200	
Miscellaneous General Expense	760	
Interest Expense	1,400	
Income Tax	51,200	
	$886,150	$886,150

Using the form provided on the following page, prepare an income statement departmentalized through income from operations.

4. *(Cont'd.)*

R-Barret Shirts and Ties

Income Statement

For Year Ended June 30, 19--

	Department S	Department T	Total
Revenue from sales:			
Sales			
Less sales returns and allowances			
Net sales			
Cost of goods sold:			
Inventories, July 1, 19--			
Purchases			
Goods available for sale			
Less inventories, June 30, 19--			
Cost of goods sold			
Gross profit			
Operating expenses:			
Selling expenses:			
Sales salaries			
Advertising expense			
Depreciation expense—equipment			
Store supplies expense			
Miscellaneous selling expense			
Total selling expenses			
General expenses:			
Office salaries			
Rent expense			
Heating and lighting expense			
Property tax expense			
Insurance expense			
Uncollectible accounts expense			
Miscellaneous general expense			
Total general expenses			
Total operating expenses			
Income from operations			
Other expense:			
Interest expense			
Income before income tax			
Income tax			
Net income			

5. *Divisional income statement and rate of return on investment analysis.*

Kakacek Company is a diversified company with three operating divisions organized as investment centers. Condensed data taken from the records of the three divisions for the year ended December 31 are as follows:

	Division P	Division I	Division C
Sales	$2,000,000	$3,000,000	$3,600,000
Cost of goods sold	1,200,000	1,950,000	2,700,000
Operating expenses	560,000	690,000	504,000
Invested assets	1,600,000	2,000,000	2,400,000

The management of Kakacek Company is evaluating each division as a basis for planning a future expansion of operations.

(a) On the form below, prepare condensed divisional income statements for Divisions P, I, and C.

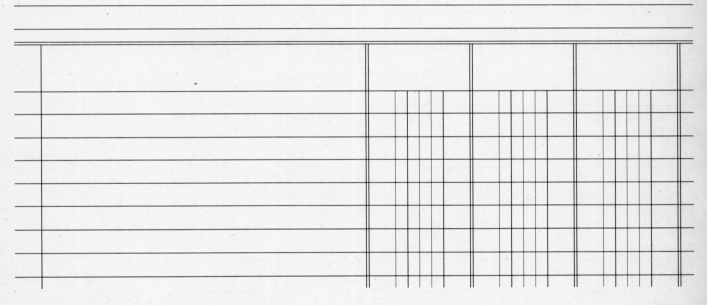

(b) Using the expanded expression, compute the profit margin, investment turnover, and rate of return on investment for each division.

Chapter 27

DIFFERENTIAL ANALYSIS AND PRODUCT PRICING

Notes from lecture and study:

_____

_____

_____

_____

_____

_____

_____

_____

_____

_____

_____

_____

_____

_____

_____

_____

_____

_____

_____

_____

_____

_____

_____

_____

_____

_____

_____

1. *Differential analysis (lease or sell).*

City Hospital has a three-year-old x-ray machine that is no longer adequate to handle the requirements of the hospital. The machine was purchased at a cost of $72,000 and has an accumulated depreciation of $30,000. McGloshen Medical Center has offered $25,000 for the machine delivered. The delivery cost would be $2,000. Dayton Clinic offered to lease the machine from City Hospital for 5 years at $10,000 per year (at which time the salvage value will be negligible). The cost of repairs, maintenance, and insurance on the machine would be $1,500 per year and would be the responsibility of City Hospital. You have been asked to advise City Hospital as to whether the machine should be leased or sold. What would be your recommendations?

Prepare a differential analysis report to support your answer.

_____

_____

_____

_____

_____

_____

_____

_____

_____

_____

_____

_____

2. *"Make or buy decision."*

Gomez Company is considering the production of a microchip it has been purchasing for $17.40 per unit. Production for the company has been running at about 75% of capacity, and no significant increase is estimated in the foreseeable future except for the production of the microchip in question (which would require about 12% of capacity).

Gomez can buy materials for the microchip at $7.60 per unit; direct labor is estimated at $6.50. Variable manufacturing overhead is 60% of direct labor cost. Fixed manufacturing overhead amounts to $220,000 at any operating level up to 100%.

Determine whether it would be better for Gomez to make or buy the microchip.

_____

_____

_____

_____

_____

_____

3. *Differential analysis for discontinuance of department.*

Following is a statement of departmental operations of Mosley's Sporting Goods for the year ended September 30, 19--.

	Dept. B	Dept. J	Total
Gross profit	$ 56,800	$204,400	$261,200
Operating expenses:			
Advertising	6,000	9,800	15,800
Rent	12,000	15,000	27,000
Utilities	8,600	12,000	20,600
Salaries—employees	26,400	39,700	66,100
Salaries—officers	15,600	25,200	40,800
Supplies	1,100	2,800	3,900
Miscellaneous	2,140	5,600	7,740
Total expenses	$ 71,840	$110,100	$181,940
Net income (loss)	$(15,040)	$ 94,300	$ 79,260

The question of eliminating Department B has arisen. For the purpose of this analysis, consider that rent, utilities, officers' salaries, and miscellaneous expenses are indirect expenses and would not be reduced if a department were eliminated; all other expenses are direct and would be reduced by the amount allocated to the discontinued department.

Prepare a schedule showing the effect of the elimination of Department B on net income.

	Current Operations			Discontinuance of Dept. B
	Dept. B	Dept. J	Total	

4. *Decision on acceptance of additional business at a special price.*

The UNT Corporation manufactures two-way radios. The company desires to submit a bid for the sale of 15,000 units to be purchased by the government of Canada. This contract will not interfere with the production or sale of the 205,000 radios now marketed in the U.S. at a price of $40 per radio.

An examination of current manufacturing costs shows that materials used for each of these radios cost $14. Labor is $9.40 per unit, and variable manufacturing overhead is $6 per unit. The fixed overhead for the plant is $410,000 a year and would not be changed if the 15,000 radios are produced.

The company officials feel that a bid of $32 per unit would be accepted.

(a) Would you advise UNT to submit a bid of $32? Explain your answer.

_____

_____

_____

_____

_____

_____

_____

_____

_____

_____

_____

(b) What, if any, will be the additional profits for UNT from the contract if accepted?

_____

_____

_____

_____

_____

_____

_____

_____

(c) What is the lowest bid that UNT can submit to earn additional profits?

_____

_____

_____

_____

_____

_____

_____

Chapter 27 (Continued)

5. *Cost-plus pricing.*

The following costs and expenses are for the Panda Manufacturing Company, which manufactures smoke detectors for the airline industry:

Variable costs and expenses:

Direct materials	$ 5.00 per unit
Direct labor	4.00
Factory overhead	2.00
Selling and administrative expenses	1.50
Total	$12.50 per unit

Fixed costs and expenses:

Factory overhead	$110,000
Selling and administrative expenses	60,000
Total	$170,000

The Panda Manufacturing Company desires a profit equal to a 15% rate of return on invested assets of $1,068,000.

(a) Total cost concept of product pricing.

(1) Determine the amount of desired profit from the production and sale of smoke detectors.

(2) Determine the total costs and expenses and the cost amount per unit for the production and sale of 200,000 smoke detectors.

(3) Determine the markup percentage for the detectors.

5. *(Cont'd.)*

(a) (4) Determine the selling price of the smoke detectors.

(b) Product cost concept of product pricing.

Assume that the Panda Manufacturing Company uses the product cost concept of applying the cost-plus approach to product pricing.

(1) Determine the total manufacturing costs and the amount per unit for the production and sale of 200,000 smoke detectors.

(2) Determine the markup percentage for the detectors.

(3) Determine the selling price of the detectors.

5. *(Cont'd.)*

  (c) Variable cost concept of product pricing.

    Based on the previous data, assume that the Panda Manufacturing Company uses the variable cost concept of applying the cost-plus approach to product pricing.

    (1) Determine the cost amount per unit for the production and sale of 200,000 detectors.

    (2) Determine the markup percentage for the detectors.

    (3) Determine the selling price of the detectors.

Notes from lecture and study:

1. *Capital expenditures and return on investment.*

Greensboro Corporation is planning an investment that will cost $9,000,000. The expected annual net income is $450,000 for an 8-year period. The annual cash flow from this investment is $2,250,000 for the 8 years. The investment will have no residual value at the end of 8 years. The company uses a 10% rate of return for discounted cash flow analysis.

(a) What is the average rate of return on the investment?

(b) Compute the cash payback period.

2. *Discounted cash flow method.*

Compute the excess or deficiency of present value over the amount invested by Greensboro Corporation using the discounted cash flow method. The present value of $1 at a compound interest of 10% for each of the 8 years will be

Year	Present Value of $1 at 10%
1	.909
2	.826
3	.751
4	.683
5	.621
6	.564
7	.513
8	.467

3. *Discounted cash flow method, discounted internal rate of return method.*

The planning committee of Buford Inc. is considering two capital investment projects. The estimated net cash flows from each project are as follows:

Year	Project 106	Project 110
1	$90,000	$60,000
2	90,000	60,000
3	90,000	60,000
4	90,000	60,000
5	90,000	60,000

Project 106 requires an investment of $269,190, while Project 110 requires an investment of $216,300. No residual value is expected from either project.

(a) Compute the following for each project:

(1) The excess (deficiency) of present value over the amount to be invested, as determined by the discounted cash flow method. Use a rate of 15% and the present value of $1 table appearing in Chapter 28 of the textbook.

(2) A present value index.

3. *(Cont'd.)*

  (b) Determine the discounted internal rate of return for each project by (1) computing a "present value factor for an annuity of $1" and (2) using the present value of an annuity of $1 table appearing in Chapter 28 of the textbook.

4. *Alternative capital investment decisions.*

The investment committee of the Nickel Company is evaluating two projects. The projects have different useful lives, but each requires an investment of $200,000. The estimated net cash flows from each project are as follows:

Year	Project A	Project B
1	$50,000	$70,000
2	50,000	70,000
3	50,000	70,000
4	50,000	70,000
5	50,000	
6	50,000	

The committee has selected a rate of 12% for purposes of discounted cash flow analysis. It also estimates that the residual value at the end of each project's useful life is $0; but at the end of the fourth year, Project A's residual value would be $100,000.

  (a) For each project, compute the excess (deficiency) of present value over the amount to be invested, as determined by the discounted cash flow method. Use the present value of $1 table appearing in Chapter 28 of the textbook. (Ignore the unequal lives of the projects.)

4. *(Cont'd.)*

(b) For each project, compute the excess (deficiency) of present value over the amount to be invested, as determined by the discounted cash flow method, assuming that Project A is adjusted to a four-year life for the purposes of analysis. Use the present value of $1 table appearing in Chapter 28 of the textbook.

(c) What advice would you give on the relative merits of the two projects?